# Praise for *Suddenly in Charge, Second Edition*

"The best advice is simple, direct, and immediately actionable. Roberta delivers on all this and more. A lifesaving guide for any new manager"!

—**Marshall Goldsmith—The international best-selling author or editor of 35 books including** *What Got You Here Won't Get You There* **and** *Triggers.*

"Matuson offers practical, no-nonsense advice for some of the most common situations leaders find ourselves managing through at some point in our careers, it's like having a coach on your bookshelf! Grab a copy for yourself, and one for a friend—they'll thank you!"

—**Sandy Rezendes, Chief Learning Officer, Citizens Financial Group, Inc.**

"Sad to say, doing your job well isn't sufficient for success. Unless you also learn to navigate critical relationships with your boss and your employees, everything else is in jeopardy. Consider *Suddenly in Charge* your lifeline, helping you make sense of the complex terrain of the modern workplace."

—**Dorie Clark, author of** *Reinventing You* **and** *Stand Out*, **and adjunct professor at Duke University's Fuqua School of Business**

"Wow! I didn't think it was possible, but the second edition of *Suddenly in Charge* is even better than the first! Roberta's no-nonsense approach is exactly what is needed in the fast-paced world of work. A must read for every manager."

—**Jay Hargis, Former Director of Learning and Development at Tufts Medical Center, and adjunct professor at NYU.**

"Roberta understands that people are the heart of any business. As a Boston based family business owner, I completely agree with her. I would highly recommend this book to leaders and anyone who heads up a business."

—**Peter Rinnig, owner QRST's**

"In *Suddenly in Charge*, Roberta does a fabulous job of weaving practical action steps with extraordinarily insightful knowledge that we all need. Having led people and organizations for over 25 years in the US Navy and various industries, I can without a doubt recommend *Suddenly in Charge* to anyone wanting to improve their leadership and followership capacity. And, as a father of three soon to enter the workforce, this will be a must read at the Koonce household! Thanks, Roberta, for sharing your wisdom!"

—**Bob Koonce, Co-Author of** *Extreme Operational Excellence: Applying the US Nuclear Submarine Culture to Your Organization*, **Former Nuclear Submarine Commander and Principal Officer, High Reliability Group LLC**

"I have personally worked with Roberta, she assisted me in evaluating and changing my team. I now have the high performing team I wanted. This book can do the same for you!"

—**Ronald Bryant, President Baystate Noble Hospital**

"*Suddenly in Charge* is a must read for both experienced and new leaders. You'll learn practical tips on how to navigate up, down and across your network and most importantly the value of strong relationships with yourself, your team, and the business."

—**Sandy Allred, Kimberly-Clark, Senior Director, Talent Management**

# Suddenly in Charge

## MANAGING UP,
### Managing Down,
### Succeeding All Around

*Revised and Updated*

ROBERTA CHINSKY MATUSON

NICHOLAS BREALEY
PUBLISHING

BOSTON • LONDON

First published in 2017 by Nicholas Brealey Publishing
An imprint of John Murray Press

An Hachette company

23  22  21  20  19  18  17     1  2  3  4  5  6  7  8  9  10

**Library of Congress Control Number: 2017012373**

ISBN 978-1-473-65605-5
U.S. eBook ISBN 978-1-857-88467-8
U.K. eBook ISBN 978-1-473-64412-0

Printed in the United States of America

Nicholas Brealey Publishing policy is to use papers that are natural, renewable
and recyclable products and made from wood grown in sustainable forests. The
logging and manufacturing processes are expected to conform to the environ-
mental regulations of the country of origin.

Nicholas Brealey Publishing
Carmelite House
50 Victoria Embankment
London EC4Y 0DZ
Tel: 020 3122 6000

Nicholas Brealey Publishing
Hachette Book Group
53 State Street
Boston, MA 02109, USA
Tel: (617) 263 1834

www.nicholasbrealey.com

# How to Navigate This Book

> *Once you've mastered **Managing UP**, **FLIP THE BOOK OVER** and begin working on the skills you will need to successfully **Manage DOWN**.*

**B**efore we begin, let's get one thing straight. **Managing UP** is not about brown-nosing, nor is it about becoming the boss's favorite. It's about learning how to work within the confines of an organization to get what you need, while helping your boss and the organization meet their objectives. It's about using influence and acting with integrity and purpose.

**Managing UP** is a skill that can be developed through practice. However, like many things in life, just when you think you've got it nailed down, the circumstances change. For example, you may have finally figured out how to best manage your boss right before being assigned a new boss. Or you may have mastered the game of office politics only to find that the board has been turned upside down and you must start again.

It's been over twenty-five years since I began practicing this skill and I still refer to the books I used when I first started fine-tuning my craft. I hope you will do the same with this book. Read it, practice, and when done, place it on your bookshelf so that you can refer to it when you most need it. Send me an e-mail at Roberta@matusonconsulting.com and let me know how your life has dramatically improved as a result of this book. Now let's begin.

*This book is dedicated to my husband, Ron, who always believed I had a book in me, and my children, Zachary and Alexis, who I hope and pray will use this book to guide them throughout their careers. And to my parents and siblings, who always encouraged me to dream big.*

# Contents

**CHAPTER THREE**

# How to Push Back and Back Down When Necessary

**CHAPTER FOUR**

# Help! My Boss Is Young Enough to Be My Child

**CHAPTER EIGHT**

# How to Work with a Coach or a Mentor

**CHAPTER NINE**

# Seven Signs Your Time Is Up

# Acknowledgments

I'd like to thank my agent, Linda Konner, who told me "no" when I didn't want to hear it and "yes" when she knew I had a book worth writing. I'd like to thank my former editorial director, Erika Heilman, for being as excited about this book as I am, and my new editorial director, Alison Hankey, for shepherding the new edition into production, and the staff at Nicholas Brealey Publishing, who successfully carried out my topsy-turvy idea of flipping this book without ever losing their balance.

My deepest gratitude goes to my mentor, Alan Weiss, who has offered guidance and support throughout my consulting practice. His push to constantly improve and his reminders for me to come back to earth have kept me grounded and moving forward.

I would also like to thank everyone who willingly shared their stories of what it was like when they were suddenly in charge, and the executives who were willing to provide a rare glimpse of what goes on inside the minds of business owners and senior leaders.

Finally, I'd like to apologize to those of you who were my first direct reports when I became suddenly in charge. As you can see, the lessons you have taught me have stayed with me for life.

# Foreword

In my twenty-five-year consulting practice with about half the Fortune 500 firms, and in coaching executives and entrepreneurs globally, I've found a fascinating phenomenon: Not enough people prepare for success!

They prepare for failure, disappointment, delay, and even cataclysm, but not necessarily for the blessings and opportunities that regularly occur in life and work. Hence, my attraction to Roberta Matuson's work and her distinctive approach to managing up and down. This book is intended to turn you topsy-turvy. How appropriate!

Volatility in the workplace is not a passing fad, temporary trend, or singular aspect of unpredictable economies. It is the new normal. As you view your career—not merely your "work" nor solely your "job"—you must assume a 360-degree view, because at any given time you may be suddenly thrust into a different part of that universe. You may emerge groggy from the wormhole, or you can emerge primed and ready for new responsibilities and differing relationships.

Relationships change based on juxtaposition. Yesterday's lunch buddy can be tomorrow's trusted lieutenant or troublesome nihilist. The earth isn't flat and neither is your professional or business universe. You will move, rotate, and revolve among others, but your alignment and realignment aren't subject to immutable laws of nature, quantum physics, or "dark matter." They are dependent upon your own preparation and energetic responsibility for new conditions and relationships. Unlike the universe, it's not uncommon for rapidly moving organizational bodies to crash and burn. Unfortunately, we all see it happen routinely.

Roberta intelligently separates her guidance into "managing down" and "managing up." In doing so, she provides unique "both sides of the desk" perspectives in areas such as corporate politics, wielding influence, credibility, trust, motivation, workplace dynamics, performance evaluations, and making tough calls. Her innovative "double mirror" enables you to watch both the front-stage actor and the backstage director at work.

Warren Bennis's seminal work, *The Unconscious Conspiracy: Why Leaders Can't Lead,* was engendered by his own stint as leader of a major university, his unmet expectations, unanticipated dramas, and failed theories. A stronger body of work about leadership emerged from that crucible.

Here, Roberta uses her career in organizations and as a consultant to provide the deft observations and analysis that grace her own contributions. She talks about her own leadership style "marinating" and uses apt analogies about marriages and therapy (or is that redundant?). The reader can't escape the feeling of having been invited behind the curtain to chat with the actors, inspect the scenery, appreciate the technical crew—and still watch the inevitable error or improvisation that takes place once the performance is underway!

*Suddenly in Charge* will help you rapidly adjust to the inexorable seismic shifts that will affect your career. Here are some points on which to be especially vigilant:

- Promotion is usually not the result of careful succession planning and lengthy preparation, but is too often traumatic and terrifying.
- The first couple of months, like the first few minutes of a speech, are inordinately important because they will determine how closely people pay attention thereafter.
- Commitment always trumps compliance, and engagement will help ensure commitment.
- You should hire and reward talent and behavior, because skills and content can always be acquired. However, it's tough for anyone to acquire enthusiasm or motivation if they are not already present.
- Trust is the *entrepôt* for credibility. And you build trust in two directions.
- Demographics constitute a legitimate force of change in the workplace, but they don't justify some people acting as "parents" dealing with "children."
- Not all relationships are worth saving. But you have to be absolutely clear on which are which.

The book is replete with this kind of hard-hitting, pragmatic, and energizing advice.

My personal experience is that people who are propelled into leadership positions, in particular, don't sufficiently appreciate that leadership is about making the toughest decisions, not about pleasing everyone (even themselves) or being a "savior." When I hear a new manager declare, "This can't happen on my watch," I know that the individual is both denying reality and avoiding unpleasant accountabilities.

You will read herein about why and how to make the tough calls, to sacrifice popularity for prudence, to avoid politics for productivity, to reward performance and not pessimism. The most difficult part of being thrust into leadership or working for a colleague now positioned as your leader is to retain the positive aspects of the former relationship while jettisoning those that are now inappropriate. Roberta is a superb navigator in helping you sail those stormy and uncertain seas.

Throughout the book, Roberta discusses the importance of respect. What I've found both in life and faithfully recorded in this work is that the assumption and sustaining of respect is a mutual need, not subject to hierarchy, size of office, or titles on a business card. Roberta deals lightly with some issues best tackled with that perspective, but always with a reverence for the individual, whether superior or subordinate. Essentially, if I were to distill her message into a sentence, as unfair as that is, I would tell you: "You can't respect others without respecting yourself."

Dealing with abrupt hierarchical and relational change is best done only if that kind of respect exists. This book helps you avoid the hubris of the quickly elevated and the chagrin of the seemingly forgotten. It creates perspective, always relying on respect for oneself and others, which is rare in modern business books but so vital in modern organizations.

Whether you read this book from front to back or back to front, whether you are the new boss or the new subordinate, you'll be better at what you do, and you'll feel elevated as a result—no matter what's on your business card.

Alan Weiss, Ph.D.
Author, *Million Dollar Consulting* and *Thrive!*;
President, Summit Consulting Group, Inc.

# Introduction to Managing Up

You may be wondering why we have chosen to begin this book with managing up, as many of you may still be in the midst of trying to figure out exactly what your new management role entails. This is the reason: If you do not *quickly* figure out how to manage up, you will not need to worry about how to manage down.

It may seem unnatural to manage those above you in the top-down world of business. But mastering this skill is *exactly* what you must do to excel in any organization. You will always have "a boss," even if you are currently an entrepreneur or you think you may be one someday. There will always be someone above you influencing what you do. This person may be your spouse, your partner, an outside investor, or may actually be your boss. It is critical to learn how to manage these relationships effectively, so you can secure the resources you need to be successful in any situation.

One of the keys to managing up is to not make it apparent that you are doing so. The only way to do this is to be authentic. If a suggestion in this book doesn't feel right for you, then tweak it until it feels like something you can wear daily. Challenge yourself to improve every day and before you know it, you will indeed be succeeding all around.

*In order to have a successful relationship with your boss you need to understand his management leadership style and adjust your behaviors, so you can give him what he needs. This will enable you to establish a productive relationship and get things done faster.*

*In my younger days, I was thrown into jobs where I wasn't the technical expert in the field. I was a plant manager, although I wasn't an engineer. I was director of sales and I had no sales or marketing experience. I soon realized that success was all about the people and aligning the department to the business.*

*I always had the point of view, "How do I help make my boss more successful?" I knew I needed to figure him or her out very quickly. Of course there are times when we may disagree, but when we walk out of the room and the decision's been made and it's not mine, I leave in alignment.*

Roger Young
*Executive Director*
*Li & Fung*

## CHAPTER ONE

# Excuse Me, Where Do I Find the Decoder Ring?

## Understanding Your Boss's Style of Management

How I long for the sixties. Back in those days, you could receive a free decoder ring inside boxes of select breakfast cereals. I can't say for sure if that ring really worked, as I wasn't allowed to venture too far outside the four walls of the playroom. But for a young child, there was something magical about that ring. Once you put it on, it felt like you could decode anything. There have been many times in my career as a manager when I wished I had kept that ring. Maybe I would have had an easier time understanding where my boss was coming from.

I'm a bit older now and am forced to live in the world of reality, where decoder rings are a thing of the past. Or are they? Consider this chapter a modern version of a decoder ring; read it carefully to unlock the hidden secrets of your boss's management style. By doing so, you will be able to adjust your expectations and communication style so you can achieve a prosperous and peaceful coexistence with one of the most important people in your life—your boss.

# Why Understanding Your Boss's Style of Management Is So Critical

Legendary management visionary Peter Drucker, author of *The Practice of Management*, wrote, "You don't have to like or admire your boss, nor do you have to hate him. You do have to manage him, however, so that he becomes your resource for achievement, accomplishment, and personal success." Although Drucker wrote this book in 1954, his words are timeless. This statement is particularly relevant for today's workers, as people are scrambling for fewer opportunities, courtesy of the downsizing that has taken place over the past several years.

Your success in the organization is completely dependent on how well you manage your relationship with your boss. Your boss has the codes to unlock doors that will remain closed if you fail to nurture this relationship. He is the one who can advocate on your behalf for more resources. He can play a critical role in linking you with key people throughout the organization, and he can also ensure that you are assigned to projects that will provide you with continued growth. And of course he is the one who can advocate on your behalf to ensure you are rewarded appropriately for a job well done.

You have to take responsibility for the development and maintenance of your relationship with your boss. No one will have more interest in making sure your relationship helps you achieve your goals than you. You may be thinking that you are just as vital to your boss's success as she is to yours, and that is somewhat true. Your boss is indeed less likely to achieve her goals without your support. However, your boss probably has other direct reports she can rely on, while you most likely have only one boss. You most certainly won't progress, or even stay employed, without your manager's support.

In *Power and Influence: Beyond Formal Authority*, John Kotter writes that developing and maintaining effective relationships with bosses involves four basic steps. These are:

1.  Get as much detailed information as possible about your boss's goals, strengths, weaknesses, and preferred working style and about the pressures on your boss.
2.  Make an honest self-appraisal about your own needs, objectives, strengths, weaknesses, and personal style.
3.  Armed with this information, create a relationship that fits both parties' key needs and styles, and one in which both you and your boss understand what is expected of you.

4.  Maintain the relationship by keeping the boss informed, behaving dependably and honestly, and using the boss's time and other resources selectively.

Cynics and people who don't know any better may assume that the only reason people put the effort into cultivating solid working relationships with their bosses is for political gain. The reality is that people work in complex organizations where their bosses are pulled in many directions. To get the attention and support you will need to succeed in your role as a leader, you will need to take responsibility for managing these relationships.

# Breaking the Code: How to Decipher Your Boss's Management Style

The problem with bosses is that no two are alike. Right about the time you've figured out what your boss needs, you get promoted. That is, you get promoted if you've done a good job of managing your boss. Otherwise, you may find yourself searching for a new job. We are also living at a time of greater diversity of bosses. With our global economy, you may have a boss who is from another country or who may actually live in that other country while he manages you remotely. Exciting? Yes. Easy to manage? Not so much.

When you work for a large company, it's quite common to be assigned to a new work group, which means another new boss to decode. Here is some advice to those who are starting out with a new boss:

1.  Don't assume anything. Don't assume that what you are thinking is an appropriate way of communicating with a new boss and that this approach is going to match his needs and style.
2.  Ask your boss how he prefers to receive communications from you. For example, does he prefer a weekly status report or would he rather meet every other week for a one-on-one? By asking this up front, you may avoid wasting time writing reports that he will never read.
3.  You need to scan your environment. Is it fast paced? Are you working for a large, multinational corporation or in an industry marked by lots of acquisitions and consolidations? Is your boss so busy that she has little time for the details and barely has time

for the facts? If so, it's your responsibility to adjust *your* communication style by providing her with a summary of the findings and recommendations of your project, rather than providing all the details.

4.  You have to test whatever you are going to recommend. What I mean by this is that you must test your conclusions with the people who are going to be using the results of your work. That information becomes your secret weapon. For example, suppose you are responsible for providing sales tools to people who will sell your products and services. You can test your results by providing a summary of the tools to the end users to find out which tools they believe will be most effective. Then, when you are presenting to senior management, casually mention a comment or two from the people who will be using the tools. This approach demonstrates that you've done your due diligence and your work is credible.

5.  Tell people what they need to know. Keep asking yourself, so what? Does this person really need to know this? If not, move on.

I recently had a conversation with a leader who works for a global organization. She shared the following with me. "I've learned over the years that you have to adapt your style to your boss and the environment you work in. For example, early on in my career, I worked as a vice president of data processing for a small advertising firm. There, my boss was located in the next office over. We had a chance to establish a trusting relationship. He saw me every day. He trusted my recommendations and was very hands off. I now work in a situation where my boss is located across the country from me and his boss is in Europe. We have little opportunity to really get to know one another. Therefore, the level of trust is not nearly as strong as it has been with my previous employers. One thing I try to do is to listen more to what they are saying. I adjust my pace. I give them time to catch up to my thinking. I give my boss small digestible chunks of information, which helps me build trust and understanding."

This leader understands that decoding her boss is one skill she will continue to fine-tune throughout her career.

# Common Types of Managers

Managers come in a variety of shapes, sizes, and styles. Here, we'll focus on four common styles you're likely to encounter in the workplace. Don't be alarmed if your boss doesn't fit perfectly into any of these categories. People often overlap, or they may move from one category to another with little warning.

Management styles can be identified by the way a manager uses authority, the way she relates to others, whether or not she encourages and values input from her people, and by the way she, as a leader, communicates.

## THE DICTATORIAL MANAGER

This style of management is also referred to as a military, or authoritative, style. The manager who follows this style gives out orders and expects everyone to fall into line, without question. He makes all the decisions about what will be done, who will be assigned which task, how the work will be completed, and when it will be completed. Employees who fail to follow directions may feel like they are being court-martialed. The more fortunate are offered an honorary discharge, more commonly referred to as "early retirement."

Common traits of managers who embrace this style are that he is the only one who knows what is going on; is always right; isn't interested in hearing other people's views; discourages dissent; may allow some discussion, then ignores what is said; closely monitors every task; does not allow others to question decisions or authority; can often be heard yelling at subordinates; and motivates through fear.

It would be great if you could run from a manager who displays this type of behavior, but not everyone has that choice. You may live in a small town where good jobs are scarce, or you may be the sole support for your family. Possibly, you may need to stick it out because you cannot be without health insurance.

I'm not going to lie and say that you are going to be able to tame this lion. I will, however, offer some advice on how you can stay in the cage without being mauled.

Survival in this situation requires that you depersonalize the matter. The reason your boss acts this way has little to do with you. It's more about him. I've learned from personal experience that situations like this can make you physically ill. You can also lose your self-esteem, which in the end will prevent you from breaking loose because your boss will have convinced you that no one else will want you. Following are some ways to manage your relationship with The Dictator:

**Pick your battles**—If you know you've got a boss who enjoys going to battle with his charges, then give him very little ammunition. If his order isn't a matter of life and death, then do what he asks. If you are lucky, he will focus his wrath on someone who isn't falling into line as easily.

**Anticipate your boss's needs**—Dictatorial bosses love to catch people making mistakes. You can avoid falling into this trap by being prepared at all times. For example, if your boss is known for walking into people's offices demanding the latest figures, have a cheat sheet on hand so you can quickly respond should you be asked to do so.

**Do your job well**—It's difficult to excel when you are working under these conditions, but that is exactly what you must do. Do a great job so that the boss spends most of her day in someone else's cubicle.

**Establish credibility**—It's going to take a longer period of time to build trust with a manager who falls into this category, but that doesn't mean it is impossible to do so. Give her exactly what she needs, when she needs it, and eventually she will cut back on the micromanaging.

## THE LAISSEZ-FAIRE MANAGER

Everyone dreams about having a manager who is completely hands off. That is, until he gets a boss who is an extreme version of hands off. Managers who fall under this umbrella communicate very little with their direct reports. They believe people will know exactly what to do through osmosis. These are the same managers who will tell you at review time you aren't meeting their expectations, even though they never told you what they were. That's why it's important to closely manage this type of boss, even if it's from afar.

A less extreme version of this type of manager will tell you what you need to know to do your job and will then get out of your way so you can do it. If this group of managers were to have T-shirts printed up they would say, "If you don't hear from me, then everything is fine!"

Traits commonly associated with hands-off managers are: Limited communication; an expectation that the people in their domain are capable of managing themselves; and a belief that their direct reports can handle their own problems with little guidance or intervention. These managers also believe in high accountability. They feel that if they are giving you this level of trust, you had best deliver. Here are some ideas on how to manage The Laissez-Faire Manager:

**Be respectful of her time**—These types of managers are typically bottom-line people. If they wanted to chitchat, they'd be more hands on. Therefore, it is important to keep your conversations brief. Think about what you want to say to this person and then cut that conversation in half. This approach will force you to be succinct, which is highly valued in this time-starved world.

**Ask questions**—With this type of boss, you are going to have to ask lots of questions, since laissez-faire bosses are either too busy to give you direction or really don't know enough about what you are supposed to be doing to provide adequate guidance. The latter isn't uncommon, particularly in cases where a manager has just been given control over a department he knows little about or has come into his position without moving up through the ranks. The first question you will need to ask is what form of communication he prefers to use when receiving and responding to your questions. Does he want you to e-mail questions as they come up? Or does he prefer you hold all questions for a weekly meeting? Would he rather you handle questions the old-fashioned way—by picking up the phone?

**Keep her informed**—Yes, I did just say that when it comes to conversations, this type of manager believes less is more. However, no one likes surprises, not even a manager who is hands off. This means the onus is on you to come to her with questions, problems, and suggestions. You have to keep your boss informed about the direction you are heading, potential problems on the horizon, and any other factors that may come back to bite you if the information comes from someone else.

**Be prepared to manage your own performance**—If you want a good evaluation (or any evaluation, for that matter), you are going to have to take control of your performance review. A hands-off manager can't possibly be aware of all the contributions you have made. That's why it is your responsibility to remind her of what you've accomplished.

Several weeks prior to your review, provide your boss with a detailed self-evaluation highlighting your contributions during the review period, as well as what you have done to meet your specific goals. Write a well-balanced review. List areas of strengths, as well as areas in which you need continued development. If you acknowledge the areas in which you are working to improve, your boss is more likely to accept your self-evaluation as a fair assessment and will most likely use this information to write her version of your performance review. Don't be surprised when the review you are asked to sign looks exactly like what you submitted!

## THE BUREAUCRATIC BOSS

These are the bosses who do everything by the rules, even if the rules don't make sense anymore. You'll most likely find these types of bosses in hierarchical organizations like government agencies, hospitals, large service firms, and established family businesses. Characteristics of bureaucratic bosses include the need to be in control and a desire for structure, systems processes, and norms. "We've always done it that way," can be heard echoing through the halls of organizations where paintings of these traditionalists line the walls. Here are ways to manage The Bureaucratic Boss:

**Learn the rules**—The best way to handle a bureaucratic boss is to learn the rules and regulations of the organization. By doing so, you will have a better understanding of the traditions that have taken hold in the organization. This approach will allow you to pick and choose your battles carefully.

**Follow protocol**—When you approach your boss about doing something, you need to show him that you've gone through the proper channels prior to coming to him for final approval. You do this by dropping names of people you have spoken to about this matter.

**Be patient**—Realize that change is slow to take hold in organizations built on the foundations of bureaucracy. You may have to wait until there is a changing of the guard before your ideas can take shape. If rules aren't your thing, consider finding an organization that is less traditional in nature.

## THE CONSULTATIVE LEADER

If you could choose the type of boss you would have, this would be the one to select. When it comes to decision making, these types of leaders involve others in problem solving and weigh the options, even though they reserve veto power. Most have strong listening skills and are good at building relationships with their people and with others in the organization. They also recognize others for their contributions. Following are some ways to manage The Consultative Leader:

**Be prepared**—You *will* be asked your opinion. Therefore, it's important that you think about how you will respond to certain questions the boss is likely to ask. Be prepared to back up your statements with evidence that supports your position.

**Be an idea maker**—Consultative bosses enjoy giving people credit for their ideas. They empower their people and delight in the successes that result. They appreciate those who come to the table with innovative ideas. Give them what they want.

**Don't take things personally**—It's easy to forget that this type of boss is not running a democracy. Anticipate that there will be times when your boss will pull rank. Support her decision and move on.

**Communicate your gratitude**—You are fortunate to have a boss like this. Every now and again, let your boss know how much you appreciate his willingness to treat you more like a peer than a subordinate.

## It Takes Two to Make a Relationship Work: How Self-Awareness Plays into the Mix

I'll be the first to admit that I wouldn't survive a day in an organization where I had to cut through a lot of red tape to do my job, nor would I flourish in a job where my manager's style was that of a dictator. I can say that because I have a fairly good idea of the type of people I respond to best.

Relationships are based on the interactions between two people. Think long and hard before accepting a position with a particular boss who has a trash can full of nameplates from those who have come before you.

Take some time to assess the type of manager with whom you feel you work best. When interviewing for positions, be observant. Keep your eyes and ears open for signs that will help you determine whether your styles will align.

## The Need for Continual Maintenance

Maintaining a good working relationship with your boss requires continual effort and constant attention. You nourish these relationships by monitoring both internal and external changes and by anticipating your boss's needs before he even knows they exist. This approach is what will distinguish you as a valuable resource, to both your boss and the organization.

## HOW *NOT* TO MANAGE YOUR RELATIONSHIP WITH YOUR BOSS

Here are five surefire ways to damage your relationship with your boss:

1.  **Fail to follow through**—Your boss has to trust that you will do what you say you will do, or there is little point in working together. Do what you promise, or, if you can't, let your boss know as soon as possible so alternate plans can be made.
2.  **Go over the boss's head**—This move will almost guarantee that your time in this job will soon be coming to an end. With the exception of situations that are illegal, it is best to try to work things out with your boss before escalating the situation.
3.  **Be disrespectful to your boss**—We've all experienced times when we would have liked to slap the boss right in front of our peers. Most likely, we would regret such a move the next day (or even the next hour). You don't have to like your boss, but you certainly do have to treat her with some level of respect.
4.  **Lie to the boss**—It's all too easy to get caught in lies, particularly in this age of social networking. An example of this is calling in sick and then announcing on your Facebook page that you are taking your daughter to the beach today. Be assured that someone, somewhere in your network, will read about this. Let's hope that someone isn't your boss.
5.  **Throw your boss over the cliff**—Your job is to support your boss. It is not to let his superiors know how inept your boss is. If you're asked about your boss's performance, you certainly don't need to lie. But you also don't need to bring out a ten-page list of all the inadequacies you've noticed since the day you started working for this person.

## KEY LEARNING POINTS

- The most important skill you will need to master is managing your boss. Your success in the organization is completely dependent upon how well you manage your relationship with your boss.

- Author and management expert John Kotter offers four basic steps for managing your boss effectively. They include gathering as much detailed information as possible about your boss's goals, strengths, weaknesses, and preferred working style; honestly assessing your own needs in terms of your personal style; using this information to create a relationship that meets the needs of both parties; and maintaining the relationship by demonstrating you are dependable, honest, and respectful of your boss's time.

- There are four main groups of management styles we are considering (although there are probably a dozen more): Dictatorial, Laissez-Faire, Bureaucratic, and Consultative. In the world of management, nothing is simple. Your boss may be a hybrid of more than one of these categories. Figure out where he fits in and then adjust your style accordingly.

- Managing your boss starts with you. You have to understand your own style of communication so that you can adapt it to the situation at hand.

- Managing the relationship with your boss is an ongoing process that requires care and attention.

*More office politics are played than you might think. It's really important to understand this and learn some coping mechanisms and self-awareness of how you will control your response. You can manage how much you will participate in office politics as well as the manner in which you participate.*

*Always look at your own motivation. Ask yourself, am I getting excited about working on a project because I'm more publicly visible or because I get to work side-by-side with the CEO, or is this the case because this project is really the right thing to do? If you start making political moves all the time that are focused only on your own success, ultimately you will not succeed.*

*It is important to understand that it is really not a zero-sum game. My success does not come at anyone else's expense.*

Paul Sartori, Ph.D.
*Former Corporate Vice President of Human Resources and Public Affairs*
*Bausch and Lomb*

## CHAPTER TWO

# Office Politics

You're in the Game,
so Deal with It!

L et's get one thing straight. No matter what you might be told, office politics is one game that is played in *every* organization. It doesn't matter whether you work for a nonprofit, government agency, private company, or family-owned business, there is always a round of politics being played somewhere, whether it's the boardroom or the back room.

Before you begin writing your letter of resignation, it's important to understand that politics isn't just about manipulation. It's about using power effectively. Jeffrey Pfeffer goes into extensive detail about this in his book *Managing with Power, Politics and Influence in Organizations* (1992). I'm a huge fan of Pfeffer's work, as he doesn't hesitate to say what others would like to sweep under the boardroom rug. I credit him with helping me decipher where the power really resided in the organizations where I was employed, which helped keep me sane during some very insane times in my business life. Without this information, you are basically working in a large gravel pit with only a small flashlight in your hand. Pfeffer shines a bright light on what really goes on in the bowels of every organization.

Pfeffer defines power as the ability to get things done through people. People who wield power effectively follow unwritten rules that allow them to maneuver swiftly through the organization to obtain scarce resources, approval of prized projects, and promotions. Learning these unwritten rules will accelerate your ability to move your career forward. Let's take a closer look at how this plays out in the real world.

## Yes, Virginia, Life Is Unfair: How Work Really Gets Done at Work

How many times have you or someone you know whined about how unfair things are at work? Maybe it appeared that someone "in the know" received a promotion you thought should have been yours. Or perhaps a colleague didn't receive funding for a project because the money went to the president's favorite department—most likely sales. Life is not fair at home and it's especially unfair at work.

I could tell you to ignore office politics at your own peril. However, I believe the following story, told by someone who learned the hard way that ignoring office politics wasn't such a great idea, has much more impact. Here's the story of Codie Sanchez, founder and CEO of Threads Redefined.

*I got lucky in this instance. I learned this lesson about office politics the hard way in my very first job in finance. I was a little girl, playing with the big boys in finance at one of the world's largest firms. I had just completed a very competitive training program and was preparing to choose my role in trading, sales, I banking, etc. However, I had an idea. I saw a chink in the armor of this goliath of a company. So I proposed a new job that would help my boss fill a role, make him look good with his bosses, and give me the international experience I craved. He loved the idea and told me to go pack my bags to be prepared after he presented to the powers that be.*

*Flash forward a few hours, I get a call to come to his office. I'm basically floating down the corridor on my own cloud nine. He sits me down and says, "I have a question for you, Codie. How do you think your colleagues view you?" Rubber screams in my head. I have no idea what he is talking about. He expands by saying, "Yes, well, it seems that your team thinks you would leave dead bodies behind you to get ahead." I'll never forget those words. Leave dead bodies. As I struggled not to tear up and find the words for clarification, he continued on. His explanation used words like intense, workaholic, I never went out to team lunches, I didn't go to group parties and my team thought my only focus was on the job. Which to be fair it was.*

*Needless to say he took my idea, created the position, and gave it to one of my colleagues, who was not apparently viewed as a serial killer. Here you have two choices; you can be a victim and complain at the injustice or you can realize that life happens for you, not to you. I chose the latter; I sat down and said to myself that apparently I had miscalculated. Perception can be reality and I have to "sell" just as hard inside my organization as I do outside of my organization. For me that meant actively softening my edges. I would plan a lunch every two months with the whole team. I would bring in cupcakes, I would Betty Crocker the crap out of it, and then I would find my own way to be me and be seen as a cultural fit. Just as in a relationship you compromise, so too must you do the same within an organization. Call it politics, call it sales, call it unfair, the moral of the story is you can be the best at your job but if you aren't seen in the right light by the right people it won't really matter.*

As a new manager, one of the first things you need to do is to look closely at how work really gets done in the organization. I'm not talking about what you may have learned during your first week of orientation, nor am I suggesting reading the company operations manual. This information is often stagnant, and in most cases represents only what the company wants you to know. I'm talking about learning how work gets done *informally*. I believe this was much easier to figure out in the fifties and sixties. Workplaces were less complicated and white men typically ran them. You could pretty much tell, based on how people looked, who the movers and shakers were. Or could you? Even back in those days, someone else often wielded a lot of power. That person was often in a position that we don't typically hear about today. They were secretaries. These women (and it almost always was a woman) made and broke many a young man's career as they controlled access into the boss's office.

Thankfully, the business world is quite different today. Women and minorities are both business owners and successful leaders. At the same time, businesses have become more complex, as companies have gone global. One can no longer use dress to determine who wears the pants in the company (thanks to the invention of business casual), nor can one make assumptions as to who the executives are based on race or gender alone.

As a new manager, you will have to fine-tune your sleuthing skills to discover how things get done informally in the organization. You do this by being observant, listening closely, and watching the way the people who seem to always get what they ask for interact with their bosses and those at the top. As you begin to understand the behavior in organizations, you will be better equipped to create and execute the game plan you will need to succeed in your organization.

## Two Types of Power

There are two sources of power in organizations. The first is position power, which is often referred to as hierarchical power. This is the formal authority someone has over others based solely on her position; this may include control of budgets and physical facilities, as well as control over information. It is interesting to note that, now that you are a boss, you too have position power, although admittedly not as much power as your boss.

The other type of power is personal power. This is the ability of the individual to influence others. The amount of personal power is directly related to the amount of trust one has established with colleagues. Consider the following: The company has instituted a company-wide hiring freeze. You don't have the position power to circumvent the freeze and bring someone new on board, as the president does. Therefore, you must rely on your personal power to convince your boss that it's in the company's best interest to approve this new hire. Your request may be granted, based on a track record of running a lean team and asking for only what you need. Another manager, one with a history of empire building, would likely have his request denied.

## Political Games: How to Avoid Checkmate

If you've ever played chess, you know you need to have a strategy going into the game if you want to win. Great chess players are constantly assessing the competition. They are trying to stay one step ahead. This is exactly the strategy you will need if you want to avoid being placed into checkmate on the job. Here's how you do this:

**Know the other players**—It doesn't take long for most people to figure out the players in the workplace who will advocate on their behalf and the ones who won't. The grapevine can provide you with information regarding people who like to see others succeed and those who would drive right over you if given the keys to a John Deere tractor.

**Think before moving**—I'm not saying that you should analyze every single move you make. However, I am suggesting that you think your moves through carefully and anticipate what might happen next, particularly when your move will affect others or when you are in a highly visible situation.

Understand that what seems like an insignificant move can come back to bite you. I recall terminating an employee who was no longer able to do his job. I ran my decision by my boss, who agreed this was the right move. Neither of us was prepared, however, for the wrath from other people in the organization who felt this employee should not have been let go. Eventually, my boss blamed me for the volcano that had erupted. He was conflict avoidant and shifted with the winds. Unfortunately, the winds were not blowing my way that day.

**Learn from your mistakes**—You don't get to be a master chess player if you don't learn from your mistakes. I see this in my home when my husband plays chess with our son. My husband is constantly remind-ing my son not to repeat a move that has cost him the game. Eventu-ally, my son will figure it out and will be teaching my husband a few moves along the way.

My son has the benefit of knowing that no matter what happens, he isn't going to be tossed out of the organization we call home. You, on the other hand, won't get as many chances. If you are lucky, you'll get some second chances, providing that your mistakes weren't life threat-ening to the organization or to your boss's reputation. Third or fourth chances are rare. That's why you had best learn from your mistakes and become a better manager because of them.

**Play quietly**—Sometimes the best way to avoid a no-win situation is to play quietly. You do this by moving around the organization, making as little fanfare as possible. You operate under the radar screen. This technique is extremely useful when you suspect your boss is going head to head with someone who appears to be much more powerful than he is, and you anticipate you'll be called into action the moment war is declared. When asked to take sides, you simply respond by saying you need some time to think about things. Hopefully, matters will blow over by the time your boss checks back with you.

# Determining the Person Who Is *Really* in Charge

I love the warning that appears on my side-view mirror, the one that says, "Objects in mirror may be closer than you think." It reminds me a lot of business. You think you know what's coming up behind you, but sometimes that situation is closer than it appears. Are you able to get out of the way before you are rear-ended? Should you accelerate or should you slow down? And what happens if, while you are watching one situation, another one cuts you off?

This is a frequent occurrence on the corporate highway, where having an extra set of eyes wouldn't be a bad thing. One minute you think you know who is in control. You invest your time in developing a relationship with those people who you believe can pave the way, only to find out they really aren't the decision makers or, as of last night, they are no longer employed by the firm.

In many organizations, especially service firms like large law and accounting firms, this scenario plays out frequently. Bernard Gore, who is currently employed as a program manager at the New Zealand Police, has worked in an environment where power plays were made every day. "I've worked in large law firms (with a hundred or more partners) where every partner believes she is the ultimate voice, and very few staff will do other than jump when told! I did pretty well in some cases by actually having the nerve to challenge a partner, but while that is useful for actually getting things done it does mean you accumulate enemies who can't tolerate any challenge to their ego, so it doesn't work well for a long-term engagement!" exclaims Gore.

As Gore experienced, working in organizations where the power runs like an overflowing river can be quite challenging. If you are a lawyer or a certified or chartered accountant, you may have little choice but to join one of these large firms, where you will have plenty of opportunity to refine your influencing skills.

To succeed in service organizations, you have to understand the dynamics that exist. Here is how it typically works in large service firms: People are hired for their functional expertise in computers, operations, administration, and so on. The managers of these functions then "sell" these people's time to the various project directors in the organization. Employees at all levels of the organization are expected to complete time sheets so their salaries can be allocated to particular projects. If you are in one of these supporting roles, you will find that your boss is constantly in a position of having to determine who will get first dibs on you. If you are servicing clients directly, you will be working with bosses who are under the gun to make sure every moment you are breathing is a billable moment. You should now have a better appreciation of the pressure that exists in these types of organizations.

As you move into higher levels of management in these firms, you will need to become an expert in negotiation and in working through conflict. The people who yield the power in service firms are the ones who have mastered these skills. Typically, they are also pretty tough skinned. Before electing to make your career at this type of firm, ask yourself the following:

- Do I enjoy working in an organization where many people will be in control of my destiny?
- Do I consider myself a fairly savvy person when it comes to dealing with office politics?
- Am I the type of person who is assertive enough to push back when necessary?
- Does this type of culture feel right for me?

Jobs in these types of environments are not for the faint of heart. How do I know this? I worked for a service firm and lasted only fourteen months. And that was a lot longer than many of my colleagues at that firm lasted. But if you are the type of person who enjoys this type of challenge, by all means, give it your all, as there are great financial rewards to be had if you succeed.

# Hot Potato, Hot Potato: How to Avoid Getting Burned at Work

The problem with politics is that one day you are in, and the next day you are out. The same holds true for managers in highly political environments. Here are some ways to avoid getting burned at work.

**Be careful where you attach your star**—It's great to be known as the director's right-hand person. That is, until the director is placed on the chopping block. You can avoid this by being your own person. Develop strong relationships with people other than your boss, preferably with individuals who are highly influential in the organization. One of the best ways to do this is to volunteer to work on a task force that includes people from other parts of the company. This will provide you with an opportunity to display your value to more than just your boss and will help you make a name for yourself that will be heard throughout the organization.

**Steer clear of gossip**—Most people seem to love gossip and enjoy watching others' lives implode right in front of them. This probably explains why reality television shows are so popular these days. Now, I don't know about you, but I certainly wouldn't want my work life to be the center of everyone's attention. The best way to avoid this is by limiting what you share with people about nonrelated work items at work, even if you did see another manager at a restaurant with someone other than his wife. You also don't need to strengthen the grapevine by giving your opinion on someone's work when you've never seen the work.

I recall a situation at one of the companies where I worked in which more than one person was vying for a top management role. Rumors were swirling about a personal relationship one of the candidates was allegedly having with a coworker. In the end, the position was awarded to this person. What do you think he did first? If you guessed it was to remove the people he knew were not his allies, you have guessed correctly.

While we are on the subject of politics and gossip, it bears noting that when it comes to gossip, you certainly don't want to be the lead story either. Keep your personal life separate from your work life and you'll be three-quarters of the way there. Do your job well, build strong relationships with those above you, around you, and below you, and you'll have nothing to fear.

**Don't believe everything you hear**—Imagine the following scenario: You think you have a fairly good relationship with your counterpart in San Diego. Then another manager tells you he heard that the San Diego manager has been blaming you for mistakes that never occurred. Rumor has it she is jockeying for the newly created district manager position that you were also hoping to get. STOP. Before you go further, ask yourself the following: Is the person who is telling me this someone who is reliable, or is he known as a gossip? How likely is it that this scenario is true? Will I damage the relationship with this person if I go to her without evidence? What will my boss think of me if I go running into his office ranting, based on a rumor?

The fact is, there will always be people positioning themselves to be next in line for promotion. Focus on looking forward and doing a good job, instead of constantly looking behind you to make sure no one is carrying a dagger. Ignore the rumors, unless you have solid evidence that a friend has now become a foe.

We started this chapter discussing the definition of power and politics, and that's exactly where we will end. It's important to remember that politics is about interacting with others and influencing them to get things done. We can and should use our power to get things done through other people. This is what effective leaders do. We will know that we've achieved success when we are able to move our ideas forward and get people to commit because we know who to talk to, we communicate clearly and respectfully, and we are able to show others how these ideas will benefit them. People trust we will do what we say. That's really how one acquires and retains power in most organizations.

## THREE WAYS POLITICS PLAY OUT IN THE WORKPLACE

*Power has consequences in organizations for resource allocations, administrative succession, and structures.*

Jeffrey Pfeffer
*Author,* Power in Organizations

Power affects:

1.  **The allocation of resources**—Resources are tightly held, particularly in challenging economic times. Yet it's difficult, and may feel impossible, to do your job effectively without resources. Think about your ability to complete business and personal objectives with fewer people, less money, and little support from those above and around you. Perhaps now you will see why it may be in your best interest to participate in this game.
2.  **Administrative succession**—You may have observed that some people seem to climb the corporate ladder rapidly. Most likely, these are the people who get things done in the organization, which makes them more valuable. They are the ones who receive promotions, along with the pay raises and other perks that typically come with advancement. The higher up in the organization you go, the more this is so. Think about the decision-making process that goes into selecting a new CEO and what happens after this person takes the throne.
3.  **Structure**—You may be wondering what structure has to do with your job as a manager. It has plenty to do with it. The design of an organization is often referred to as the structure. In larger or more formal organizations, organizational charts are often used to depict the structure. Think about where people are located on the organizational chart and you will see what I mean. Those closer to the person holding the most power (the CEO, president, or owner) have access to better information. They also have more formal authority and nicer offices!

--------------------- KEY LEARNING POINTS ---------------------

- Office politics are played in *every* organization. It doesn't matter whether you work for a nonprofit, government agency, private company, or family-owned business. There is always a round of politics being played somewhere, whether it's the boardroom or the back room.
- Politics isn't just about manipulation. It's about using power effectively to move people and initiatives forward.
- Author and management expert Jeffrey Pfeffer defines power as the ability to get things done through people. Following the unwritten rules of wielding power will allow you to maneuver swiftly through the organization to obtain scarce resources, approval of prized projects, and promotions, which will accelerate your ability to move your career forward.

- As a new manager, one of the first things you need to do is to look closely at how work *really* gets done in the organization. This means learning how work gets done *informally*. You do this by being observant, listening closely, and watching the way people who seem to always get what they ask for interact with their bosses and those at the top.

- There are two types of power. The first is position power, which is the formal authority you are granted based on your position. This may include controlling budgets and physical facilities, as well as controlling information. The second type of power is personal power, the ability of an individual to influence others. The amount of personal power is directly related to the amount of trust one has established with those one is interacting with.

- You can avoid winding up in political checkmate by taking time to assess the other players, thinking twice before making your next move, and learning from your mistakes.

- Sometimes the person you think is in charge isn't the one who is making the decisions. You need to figure this out early on, so you can establish solid relationships with the people who really have the power to make things happen.

- You can avoid getting burned at work by not attaching yourself to someone who may be gone tomorrow, steering clear of gossip, and considering all factors before moving forward based on information heard through the rumor mill.

*Most bosses say they want people who will push back, but in reality, I'm not sure this is true. They do like an occasional disagreement. However, it's hard enough to make decisions, so when people are pushing back all the time, it just makes their life harder.*

*As the one doing the pushing, you have to make up your mind about what battles are worth fighting. If it's critical and could impact the company, then push back. If it's about whether or not coffee should be served in the office until 10:00 A.M. or 10:15 A.M., then it's probably not worth pushing back.*

*Pick your battles carefully. Choosing the wrong battle can get you fired.*

Richard Moran
*President*
*Menlo College*

## CHAPTER THREE

# How to Push Back and Back Down When Necessary

The boss is always right! Well, not exactly. Bosses are busy people with a ton on their plate. They don't have time to double-check work or examine all aspects of every situation that comes across their desk. Consequently, there are times when the boss is wrong. In these situations, you may need to tell your boss that an assumption or decision is incorrect.

When and how you do this will determine the fate of your future. However, in many cases saying nothing isn't much of an option either, especially if doing so will put people in harm's way. Take, for instance, the recent Wells Fargo fiasco, which revealed that employees were opening up accounts for unsuspecting clients without their knowledge. While it's unlikely that you'll be faced with decisions about a billion-dollar fraud, it's certainly a possibility. To help you decide what's right for you, let's take a look at what's at stake.

## Common Myths about "Yes" People

There are a number of myths about "yes" people that need to be dispelled. Here are three.

1.  **Bosses love employees who always say yes.** Well, no, that's not quite accurate. People who say yes all the time don't add much value. Imagine for a moment asking one of your employees, who happens to fit the demographic profile that your company tar-

gets, if she thinks the introduction of a new product would be well received in the marketplace. She enthusiastically says, "Yes!" even though she is actually thinking, "There's no way any of my friends or I would *ever* purchase this item."

You'd be hard pressed to convince me that this kind of a yes is preferable to an honest response that would give your boss pause—especially one that might save millions or even billions of dollars. The majority of bosses I know prefer to surround themselves with people who can think for themselves and have the courage to speak their mind.

2.  **"Yes" people are promoted more rapidly.** If you find this to be true in your organization, then you have to ask yourself if you want to spend the rest of your life surrounded by people who are parroting the boss, or if you prefer to be working in a more stimulating environment, where push-back and the presentation of new ideas are encouraged and rewarded.

    Based on my own experience, I believe that if you offer a candid view, even one that is not a popular opinion, you will gain more respect from those above you (and around you) than if you agree simply because you believe that's what's expected. When you say what's on your mind, you allow others to see that you have original thoughts. When it comes to company promotions, people who can think on their feet and make difficult decisions tend to win out over those who say "yes" just so they can fit in.

3.  **Everyone likes people who go with the flow.** I don't know about you, but I can't stand these people. I prefer people who have an opinion and say what they mean—people with a backbone. Overall, "yes" people aren't really much fun to be around; they are only a good match for the kind of person who likes to dominate every situation.

    Life is too short to go with the flow. Stop the flow or go against the flow, if need be. This approach will serve you well in business because businesses want to move their organizations forward. None are satisfied with the status quo. If you aren't pushing back, trying new things, and failing, then you aren't moving forward.

# Why People Find It Difficult to Push Back at Work

Raise your hand if you like conflict! I'm guessing most of you did *not* raise your hand. This whole idea of pushing back and making waves seems to be a challenge for many. Here's why.

## FEAR

You may be afraid that you won't be liked if you challenge other people's ideas or, worse, that your boss will fire you if you choose to challenge him. Snap out of it! You can't live your life worrying about things that in all probability won't happen. Instead, step back and evaluate whether your fears are valid or not. Chances are, you're allowing yourself to be swayed by your active—but false—imagination.

Consider the following scenarios. First, let's say your boss assigns a project to you, along with detailed instructions as to how she wants you to proceed. You begin the assignment and quickly realize you can provide the same results in half the time. You tell her so. Is your boss angry with you for pushing back on her instructions and giving her a better outcome? Does she kick you to the curb? Of course not!

Now let's say a coworker shares an idea with you and asks you for your opinion. You give the idea consideration and then push back on some assumptions you think are incorrect. Is this the last time you and your coworker speak? Does he stop inviting you to lunch? No. In all likelihood, it's still just business as usual.

The next time someone says something that you don't agree with, take a stand. Make yourself do this each time it is needed, and over time you will find that it feels natural to do so.

## LOW SELF-ESTEEM

I've coached hundreds of leaders, and I have found that many people have self-esteem issues. They care way too much what other people think about them. At times, they act as if the other person has a gun in hand and will use it if they do something to offend him. Of course, when you first read this, you will probably think, "That's ridiculous." However, after further consideration, you may realize that perhaps this is hitting just a little bit too close to home for you. Relax. No one is shooting at you.

Self-esteem is about self-worth. It's about having the honest belief that you are good at what you do and that you deserve to be where you are. It's about the language you use and how you show up each day. It's about operating from a position of strength, as opposed to the fear I just wrote about.

Self-esteem is a vital trait of success. After all, if you don't believe in yourself, why would anyone else? The next time you sense that your lack of self-esteem is getting in the way of doing what you know needs to be done, consider changing your internal and external language. Instead of saying, "If I tell her I think she is wrong, she will fire me," say, "I'd be remiss if I didn't tell her that she is about to drive off a cliff."

## PEER PRESSURE

In some organizations, the culture is such that pushing back is *verboten*. Two examples of this are the now-defunct Enron, which imploded as a result of illegal accounting practices that went on for years before someone finally decided to push back and blow the horn, and Volkswagen, which admitted that 11 million of its vehicles were equipped with software that was used to cheat on emissions tests. Clearly what happened at VW wasn't the work of one person. Many people knew and chose to push ahead, rather than push back.

I'm not going to lie to you and tell you that it's easy to be the one person who is willing to call out bad behavior that is considered acceptable behavior in organizations where ethics are in short supply. It's not. However, at the end of the day, you need to be able to look yourself in the mirror and like what you see.

# How to Stop Saying Yes When You Want to Say No

All of us can remember a time when we said yes to our boss when we really wanted to say no. When I was the director of human resources for a commercial real estate company, I accepted a request from my boss that had nothing to do with my job. He asked me to cohost a chili cook-off at one of our shopping centers. I didn't think I could say no, so I said yes. In hindsight, I was not prepared for what turned out to be an epic event.

You've probably heard that everything is bigger in Texas, and this cook-off was no exception. For months, I spent every evening and weekend leading up to the cook-off with my staff by my side, making sure we had the perfect recipe for a successful event. The cook-off was a huge triumph, but not without a cost. I lost sight of the fact that my staff had a life outside of work. My inability to say no put undue pressure on my team. If I had it to do it over again, I would find a way to contribute to the day without being all in. Here are some examples of common scenarios where, like me, you may feel compelled to say yes, and what to say instead.

## WHEN YOU DON'T HAVE THE TIME OR CAPACITY TO TAKE ON MORE

Suppose your boss assigns more work to you and you don't have any bandwidth left. Saying, "I don't have time," seems like an honest response when you are up to your eyeballs in other work, but this approach may cause your boss to question your ability to multitask and execute the assignments he's already given you.

A better response would be to say, "I need your help prioritizing my projects." Then be prepared to lay out what's currently on your plate, along with an estimate as to how long it's going to take to complete these items and what you may have to put aside in order to honor his new request.

The best thing about this approach is that you aren't saying no, nor are you agreeing to take on work that you won't be able to complete in a way that is satisfactory to your boss. You are also reminding him how much he's assigned to you and allowing him to pick which task takes priority. In the end, he may decide to assign this project to a coworker whose plate has more room than yours.

## WHEN YOU DISAGREE WITH THE ASSIGNED APPROACH

You wouldn't follow someone's driving directions knowing you were about to hit a dead end, right? Sometimes your boss will tell you to do something that you know won't end well. You may be tempted to say, "Are you *kidding* me? I would never take that approach with this customer!" However, let me suggest a response that is less abrasive: "With your permission, I'd like to suggest another idea."

In all likelihood, your boss will say yes, and you'll have an opportunity to present your idea for her consideration. And since she's agreed to hear what you have to say, in all likelihood she will be open to changing her mind or at least meeting you in the middle.

If she says, "No, this is the way we are going to do this," then you have two choices. You can do what you've been asked to do. Alternately, if doing so would put people in harm's way, you can say, "I'm very concerned about this," and then tell her why. Hopefully, she is usually open to suggestions. If not, then consider if in the long run she is the right boss for you.

## WHEN YOU BELIEVE YOUR BOSS IS ABOUT TO MAKE A COSTLY MISTAKE

Like you, your boss is probably working on a number of initiatives simultaneously. But what if you spot a major misstep that your boss is about to take just as the project is nearing completion? You might say, "I'm not doing this because you are about to make a *very* expensive mistake," but this may give him the impression that you are challenging your boss's smarts.

A better way to get his attention without setting off all the alarms would be to say, "You know, I've been reviewing the numbers on this equipment we are about to buy, and I am wondering if we may have overlooked something. Can we talk about this before proceeding?" Most likely he will respond by asking what exactly you think has been overlooked.

If he decides to proceed without hearing your concerns, then be sure to note in your calendar that you tried to warn him, just in case the situation comes back to bite him—and possibly you as well.

## WHEN THERE'S A VALID REASON TO DENY THE REQUEST

Let's say that you are working on putting the finishing touches on a presentation that will be used to pitch a new client. Suddenly someone realizes the printer is out of ink. Your boss looks around the room and assigns you the task of going to Staples to pick up more ink. You don't want to do this because stopping your work to shop for ink will interrupt your creative juices. However, if you simply say, "No, I don't want to do this," you'll come across as someone who doesn't play well with others.

If you truly believe that stopping to do this task will have a negative impact on the outcome of your project, consider responding with, "Perhaps someone else can run over to Staples, so I can use this time to incorporate the last-minute changes to our client pitch that we've all agreed to include."

Of course, if you're simply annoyed that your boss always selects you, but following the boss's order won't really impact your project, then it's probably wise just to do it. At a later time, you can decide if it's worth raising this issue with your manager so that mundane tasks can be distributed more equally in the future.

## Signs It's Time to Back Down After Pushing Back

Sometimes we can get so passionate about an idea, we don't recognize the warning signs that indicate when we are about to push our boss's back to the wall. Here are some signs that you are about to go too far, and some advice about how you can pull yourself back.

**Your boss seems annoyed.** Most of the time your boss welcomes discussions regarding ongoing projects—today, not so much. You feel compelled to point out the holes in the new branding strategy that he's asked you to implement. His responses to your feedback are curt, and his constant sighing indicates you've gone from helpful to annoying in a nanosecond. His mind is made up. Your boss expects you to implement his plan. One day, you'll be the one who gets to decide the strategy. However, today isn't that day. Do what you are asked to do.

**Your boss refuses to discuss the topic anymore.** You're still not convinced your boss is taking the team in the right direction. You start to express your doubts, but in the middle of the discussion she abruptly says, "Thanks." Then she walks away. You begin to follow her, but her body language indicates she is done with this conversation. Trailing her around the office in an effort to continue the conversation will do more harm than good. Take a sharp left at the employee kitchen before she notices that you are stalking her.

**Your boss's blood pressure is rising (and so is yours).** You're in a heated conversation with your boss when you notice red blotchy spots appearing on her neck. Her voice rises as she tells you for the third time she has no interest in discussing this topic anymore. Clearly she means business. It's time to give it up. Walk away, before you say something you may regret.

**You discover you've taken the wrong stand.** Oops! You suddenly realize you've made a mistake. Of course, you wish you had come to this conclusion last week, prior to pushing your boss to give more consideration to an idea that you now believe won't work. Go back to your boss and let her know that, after further reflection, you agree with her decision. Then ask her what she needs from you in order to move forward.

**A final decision has been made.** There will be times when your boss is given a directive by his boss and is expected to carry it out. An example of this would be the decision to reduce headcount. Your boss may not be in full agreement with this decision, but he knows he needs to do what's been asked. He tells you this decision has come down from the top of the organization and asks you to prepare your list. This is not the time for you to push back. Return to your desk and work on your list.

# How to Take a Stand and Ensure It Won't Be Your Last

Leadership requires the courage to take a stand. It also requires the smarts to know when and where to do so to ensure that the stand you are about to take won't be your last. Here are some common mistakes people make when pushing back, and how to avoid them.

### PICK THE RIGHT BATTLES

One time my boss came to me with an idea he had for a new employee benefit. I wasn't convinced his idea would fly. Then he told me he heard about this from a trusted adviser. When I heard the words *trusted adviser*, I knew right then and there that he expected me to implement this idea and to do so without further discussion. After all, this recommendation came from someone he highly respected.

There are going to be lots of times when you disagree with your boss. There will also be situations that—regardless of how convincing you may be—you'll never win. Choose your battles wisely, as you have a limited amount of ammunition. You don't want to shoot off all your ammo at once on something that in retrospect isn't all that important.

### CHOOSE YOUR TIMING

I've seen many a leader implode right in front of my eyes because an employee chose an inappropriate time to push back. For example, it would be poor timing to challenge the boss's assumptions in a room filled with his peers or to profusely disagree with your boss in front of a customer.

It's *never* a good idea to embarrass your boss. Always scan your environment before advancing and going head-to-head with your boss; be sure that what you are about to say is appropriate given who else is within hearing distance. It's also advisable to take into consideration what your boss may be facing on a personal level. For example, if he just told you his spouse asked for a divorce, it's likely that what you are about to say regarding a work-related matter can wait a day or two.

## REMEMBER: LOCATION, LOCATION, LOCATION

At times, I've stood in amazement as employees took on their bosses in places that were completely inappropriate. Examples of this include in restrooms, in conference rooms filled with other staff members, and on the retail floor in full view of customers.

Don't make this amateur mistake. Nothing is so important that you can't wait until you can get to a place that offers privacy before taking your stand.

## PAIR THE RIGHT MESSAGE WITH THE RIGHT TONE

The tone of voice that you use in your verbal communication influences how others interpret your message. You may be perfectly correct in what you are about to say to your boss. However, if your tone is inappropriate, none of this will matter. For example, bosses rarely appreciate a sarcastic tone or a loud, overbearing voice.

Email communication can get even stickier. Lots can get lost in translation. When using email to push back on an idea with your boss, write your email, set it aside. and review it one more time later before hitting the send button.

──────────── KEY LEARNING POINTS ────────────

- There will be times when your boss is wrong, which means there will be situations in which you'll need to tell your boss that an assumption or a decision is incorrect. Leadership requires the courage to take a stand and to push back when necessary.
- There are a number of incorrect assumptions about "yes" people, which need to be dispelled. Bosses are *not* looking for "yes" peo-

ple, as these individuals add very little value. Nor do they prefer people who go with the flow. Managers appreciate employees who have minds of their own and are willing to step forward and challenge the status quo, all in the name of improving the client's condition.

- There are a number of reasons people don't push back. Fear of how they will be perceived, lack of self-esteem, and peer pressure are all factors that stop people from saying what's on their mind. It's time to get over what's holding you back and move your career forward.

- It's a lot easier to say yes than it is to say no. If you continue down this path, you'll fill your life with things you don't really want to be doing. Practice telling people no. Once you get the hang of it, you'll gain control over your life.

- Sometimes we get so passionate about an idea we don't recognize the warning signs indicating we are about to push our boss's back to the wall. Rising blood pressure, a boss who looks annoyed, and a boss who refuses to engage further in a conversation with you about a related matter are all signs it's time to back down after pushing back.

- Leadership requires the courage to take a stand as well as the smarts to know when and where to do so in order to ensure that the stand you are about to take isn't your last. Make sure you choose your battles wisely, pay attention to the timing, and do so in private to make sure you don't embarrass your boss.

*When you are supervising people who are younger, it's easier. There is a general acceptance that you know what you are doing because you are older. Understand that it is more difficult for a younger person when they are supervising people who are older, because they are always having to prove themselves.*

*Give the person a break. Leadership traits are leadership traits, regardless of age. Let young managers show you what they are capable of. Help them learn the business. Cut them some slack. You have a lot to offer one another. Reach out to them. Help them.*

*You have a responsibility to teach your boss. You make your boss successful, you become successful. Your boss fails, you fail. If the person is arrogant, regardless of age, go get another job because it doesn't work.*

Frank Guidara
*Former CEO*
*UNO Chicago Grill*

## CHAPTER FOUR

# Help! My Boss Is Young Enough to Be My Child

Strategies on How to Manage a Younger Boss

I t's official. Younger people have taken over the office. As seasoned workers continue to delay retirement, this scenario will become the rule rather than the exception. A recent AARP survey found that nearly 70 percent of employed fifty- to seventy-year-olds planned to work during what they view as their retirement years. That means more and more workers will answer to bosses who are decades their junior. In fact, according to a 2002 study by the Families and Work Institute, 71 percent of workers fifty-eight years old and older had significantly younger supervisors.

It happens to the best of us. You may one day wake up and find you are among the older workers in the office, or you may be returning to the workplace to find that your contemporaries are no longer in charge. In either case, how well you manage this situation will have a direct impact on your level of job satisfaction as well as your ability to succeed in the organization. Therefore, it is worth taking the time to learn how to manage these relationships. Having a roadmap to help navigate through this new territory can help you avoid many of the pitfalls that derailed those who came before you. Your situation doesn't have to spell disaster if you are willing to make some adjustments.

# Give Your Boss a Chance

Did you know that some of the most popular children's book authors—Dr. Seuss, Louisa May Alcott, Margaret Wise—never had children? Their lack of experience as parents didn't interfere with their ability to write books that resonated with kids. And just because your boss doesn't have years of experience under his belt doesn't mean that he won't go down in history as one of the best bosses you've ever had.

Frank Guidara, former CEO of national restaurant chain UNO Chicago Grill, believes good leadership is good leadership, regardless of age. UNO Chicago Grill hires people with strong leadership traits and provides training to help managers build strong leadership skills. He encourages mature workers with younger bosses to give the person a break. "Let them show you what they are capable of before passing judgment," advises Guidara.

Caryn Starr-Gates, owner of Stargates Business Communications—a copywriting shop that supports advertising, marketing, and public relations campaigns located in Fair Lawn, New Jersey—did exactly what Guidara recommends. Fifty-two-year-old Starr-Gates, who had formerly worked in the industry, jumped back into the world of full-service PR to work with a thirty-two-year-old boss, who was also the owner of the agency. Starr-Gates, who met her boss at a networking event, quickly saw that his vision for the firm aligned with hers. She jumped onboard and never looked back.

Starr-Gates believes that their relationship worked because they approached work on a level playing field. "We simply didn't view each other as adversaries," states Starr-Gates. Rather than assuming her boss was inexperienced, Starr-Gates embraced the fact that her younger boss actually knew more about certain matters than she did. She has positioned herself in the firm as a "wise voice of counsel," a strategy she recommends to others who find themselves in a similar situation.

It is easy to make judgments based on looks. We do it every day. But how often are our assumptions wrong? Here are some ideas you can use to get to know your boss:

**Listen more and talk less**—It is hard to get to know someone if you are doing most of the talking. Take some time to observe this person in action and hear what she has to say before forming an opinion. After all, isn't this exactly what you would like your boss to do?

**Set up an informal meeting with your boss**—The pressures of work can be overwhelming, particularly for younger people who are still trying to make their mark. The behavior you see when someone is under pressure is very different from what you may observe in a more informal setting. A good way to get to get to know your boss better is to set up an informal meeting.

Ask your manager if he would be willing to meet you off-site for coffee or for lunch at a local restaurant so that you are both free from office interruptions. Use this time to get to know your boss. Ask specific questions that will provide insight into what your boss values. For example, does he like frequent communication or does he prefer to receive weekly updates? Does he want to know all the background information or only your final recommendation? Be mindful of your tone when asking these types of questions. The last thing you want to do is come across as an investigative reporter doing an interview for *Dateline NBC*!

**Use the Internet**—You can bet your boss has already done a search using your name, so why shouldn't you do the same? This is a great way to gain more insight into his educational background and professional experience outside your firm. While searching, do your best to ignore any photos or information you may find on sites that have nothing to do with work, such as Instagram or Facebook. You can hope that your boss has done the same!

**Ask your boss for feedback**—A younger boss may find it difficult to provide a more experienced worker with feedback. Therefore, you may find yourself in the uncomfortable position of not quite knowing where you stand in terms of your performance. This means that you may need to be the one who initiates this conversation.

Begin by asking your boss to provide you with specific feedback regarding your performance. Ask him how well you are meeting his expectations on specific projects and what you can do to better align your goals with his goals. Ask him to identify the areas in which he thinks you excel and those you might be able to improve. Allow your boss to mentor you in those areas where he or she really does know more than you do!

# Find the Middle Ground

It is only natural for conflict to occur when people who come from different backgrounds work together. Expect conflict to emerge, and manage it before things implode. Some conflict can be good. It inspires us to think about other points of view that we may not have considered. This in turn allows us to create new ways of doing things. However, too much conflict can be destructive to both the organization and your career. That's why it is important to find the middle ground.

One of the biggest mistakes Caryn Starr-Gates, director of communications at The DSM Group, has seen her contemporaries make is to push back too hard on matters relating to technology. Though she still pines for her IBM Selectric typewriter, Starr-Gates knows that companies have long since moved on. "Making technology a battleground is a big mistake," notes Starr-Gates. "It's okay to not be comfortable or say you are not comfortable, but don't make it an issue. Relax. Learn it. Don't make it be us against them. And never say, 'We didn't have to do it that way before. . . .'"

Let's say that you are a Baby Boomer (born between 1946 and 1964) and your boss is a Gen Xer (born between 1965 and 1979). You have just received news that your department will be going through a major software conversion next month. Your boss doesn't think this is a big deal, since she can learn a new software program just by placing the manual on her forehead. You, like many Boomers, require hands-on training. Simply telling your boss this will most likely result in little being done to improve your situation. However, by presenting several options for her consideration, you may get exactly what you need. Here is a sample script of how you might go about this:

> Anne, I know a transition is coming. All of us on the team are onboard with the change. But some members of the team, including myself, may need more support than the manual can provide. I'm wondering if you would consider some hands-on training. By that, I mean sending us to a course before the conversion, or perhaps you would be willing to conduct a few short sessions either before or after work, for those of us who need this type of support. By doing so, you will be guaranteed a smooth transition and you will be freed up to work on the high-profile acquisition project.

This approach provides a way for you and your boss to meet in the middle. After all, you both want to see the project succeed. Together, you are aligning your differences to accomplish mutually agreed goals, without you telling your boss she is too young to understand that not everyone learns the same way. Who wouldn't honor this request?

## Acknowledge Differences and Move On

Let's face it. You and your younger boss may have grown up in two different worlds, but this doesn't mean that you can't coexist peacefully. Some differences are because of age, while others are a result of different management styles that have no direct correlation to your dates of birth.

Attorney Orrin R. Onken of Fairview, Oregon, who at the age of fifty worked for a boss twenty years his junior, believes it is important to acknowledge these differences. When asked to elaborate on this, Onken stated, "Acknowledge that you may not see eye-to-eye based on the differences in your value system. However, we can benefit each other because of these differences, rather than cause each other difficulty." In an article written by Onken titled "Surviving the Younger Boss," Onken notes that he has a very good understanding of where his thirty-year-old boss is coming from because at one point in his life, he shared similar values. "He is energetic, ambitious, aggressive, and acquisitive," writes Onken about his boss. "He is directed toward concrete, immediate goals and has a literalness of thought that leaves little room for subtlety, self-examination, or the contemplative pursuits. He secretly thinks that being a workaholic is an admirable quality and that the experience of his generation is qualitatively more dynamic than that of generations before him." Onken goes on to say that he doesn't share these beliefs, but he fully understands them, as he too held these values as a younger man.

Acknowledging differences and openly discussing ways you can meet in the middle is advice worth following, even if you are not in this particular situation. It sure beats the alternative of dancing around issues that are clearly not going to go away on their own.

## Tune Up Your Vocabulary

Going down memory lane with people from your generation may be fun, but constant reminiscing can be annoying to people who can't relate. Remember what it felt like every time your father told you how in his day he walked five miles to school in the snow? Well, that's exactly how a younger boss feels when you constantly remind her of how life was 'back in the day.' Delete the following phrases from your vocabulary: "In my day," "When I was in charge," "We tried that once," "We've never done it that way," and anything else that makes you sound like you have traveled this road before. You are no longer in the driver's seat. For this leg of the journey, you are a passenger.

Given all of today's learning options, there are no longer any excuses for failure to keep up with changes in technology. Enroll in an online course, attend a class at your local community college, or bribe your ten-year-old to tutor you on weekends. Just do something!

## Be an Employee, Not a Parent

It's easy to forget that, even though your boss looks young enough to be your child, she is *not* your child. Resist the urge to parent your boss. By that I mean, don't begin conversations with, "Well, sweetie," or, "In my experience." This may make your boss feel like she is being given directions by a parent or by someone who thinks she knows more than the boss. When asked for your opinion, be brief in your response and wait until you see a signal that indicates your boss would like to hear more before providing details.

The saying that "actions speak louder than words" is especially true when parenting gestures creep into the situation. I have firsthand experience with this (and I do mean hand!). When I started out in management, I had a secretary (yes, there were secretaries in those days) who, when she felt frustrated, would point her finger at me as if she were scolding her child. I suppose it wasn't entirely her fault, as she had a child who was my age. However, I resented being treated like a kid, particularly by someone who wasn't my mother. This gesture certainly affected our ability to work well together. Years later, we joked about this, as she hadn't even realized she was doing it!

Put your pointer finger in your holster and leave it there. The last thing you want to do is inadvertently wave your finger in your boss's face as you make your point.

Advice regarding personal matters, even if requested, should be avoided at all costs. Sure, you may have fixed your daughter up with her fiancé, but that was at home. This is work. If matchmaking is truly your calling, then perhaps it is time to apply for a job where you can do this full time.

# Bridge Communication Differences

Awareness about communication differences among those from different generations is the first step toward bridging these gaps. This is especially important when you are working with a boss who is from a different generation. To make this relationship work, you will need to understand your manager's communication style and adapt your style accordingly. For example, as a Baby Boomer, you may prefer to talk by phone or face to face. Most Gen Xers prefer e-mail. If your boss is a Millennial (born after 1980), you might give yourself a quick lesson in text messaging. This story, about a Boomer who adapted in order to communicate with her own children, illustrates exactly why you must be the one to adapt and not vice versa.

On a recent flight back from California, I sat next to a woman who appeared to be a Baby Boomer. When we landed, she took out her phone and started Snapchatting. Impressed by her speed, I politely asked her if she was messaging someone. "Indeed," she said. I told her how impressed I was, considering that I was still learning how to send simple texts. She replied by telling me that she found out a long time ago that if she wanted to communicate with her children she would need to learn how to do so on their terms.

I will never forget that conversation, as I learned a lesson that is not taught in management classes. Sometimes, you are the one who has to change. Keep in mind that the goal is to communicate effectively with your boss, not be his parent.

# Play to Win

Let's be honest. Who wouldn't feel threatened by someone who has significantly more experience and knowledge? Your boss has probably watched enough episodes of *The Office* to know there are team members just waiting in the wings for their leaders to make a mistake, so they can pounce on their jobs. This makes for great television, but sometimes it is hard to draw the line between fiction and reality.

If you are a Gen Xer or older, you probably recall the television show *Ally McBeal*. For those of you too young to remember, McBeal, played by Calista Flockhart, was a twenty-something attorney whose impact on corporate America can still be seen today. Hemlines in the workplace became at least two inches shorter, as young women tried to emulate Ally's look. As a result of this show, women across America were wearing outfits that looked great—even if sitting down comfortably was a challenge!

Much of what we believe about the workplace is shaped by what we see on television. However, television is not going to teach you how to ease the tension that may be building with your younger boss. That's because there is simply not enough drama in it, even though you may feel your office situation would make a great sitcom.

### HERE ARE FIVE THINGS YOU CAN DO TO COME OUT AHEAD:

1. Onken believes that your boss is probably as nervous as you are about the situation. He suggests that, early on, you go in and ask for advice. "Everyone loves that," states Onken. This will also make it clear that you understand who is in charge. "Fear creates defensiveness and heavy-handedness," Onken says. By eliminating the threat, you make it easier to build a relationship with your boss.

2. If you have little interest in your manager's position, tell her so. This approach will enable your boss to see you as an ally, rather than a predator.

3. If you are interested in moving up, seek your manager's assistance. Ask your boss to put together a development plan to help you transition to the next level. Appeal to his own self-interest. Remind your boss that companies are more apt to promote an employee if there is someone else in the organization who can take on his role.

4. If your boss looks good, you look good. Working together is in the interest of both parties. Keep this in mind as you are finding your way with your boss.

5. Speaking of promotions . . . if, after giving it a go, you realize that the distance to a meeting of the minds is too far to travel, then perhaps it's time to take another route. Do whatever you can to get your boss promoted. With a little luck, you will have an easier time relating to his replacement.

## Humor Goes a Long Way

Don't underestimate the power of humor in the workplace. Onken states that humor got him through a lot of tough situations when he was working with his younger boss, and it has had a long-lasting impact on their relationship. It has been a number of years since Onken has worked for this boss, but he still considers him a friend.

Starr-Gates used humor to alleviate what could be potentially stressful situations at work. She joked with her boss and coworkers about her early agency days when computers came into the workplace. "The machines took up an entire room!" exclaimed Starr-Gates. Her boss and her coworkers appreciated the fact that she was willing to share her experiences in the workplace, which occurred before they were even born! Her sense of humor and her youthful attitude allowed her to shine in an industry where you are considered over the hill by age forty.

## Get Onboard or Take a Different Route

We don't get to pick our family, nor do we get to pick our bosses. If you want this to work, and you want to be valued for what you know and what you can contribute, you have to make perfectly clear from day one that you are happy to be on your boss's team, that you will do everything you can to assist him in the transition, and that you are invested in making your boss successful. If this is not true, either don't accept this job or begin looking for a new job. If you sit at your desk and stew for the next five years (assuming you aren't tossed out of the organization), you will only be harming yourself.

If you take away only one thing from this chapter, let it be that managing a younger boss is more about managing one's attitude. In your lifetime, you will see many bosses come and go. The only constant is you. You have the ability to create your own path to success by using the tips in this chapter.

Lastly, there is of course the age-old problem of lousy bosses, which really has nothing to do with age! It's easy to place blame on what we can see. When things are not working out with our boss, we may automatically place blame on factors like age. But sometimes a problem boss is just that. It is someone who, regardless of age, should not be in a leadership position. We'll discuss this further in the chapter that follows.

───────────── KEY LEARNING POINTS ─────────────

- At some point in your career you may find yourself working for someone who is young enough to be your child. How well you manage this situation will have a direct impact on your level of job satisfaction as well as your ability to succeed in the organization. Therefore, it is worth taking the time to learn how to manage these relationships.

- Give your boss a chance to prove herself before passing judgment. In most cases, managers have been put into leadership roles because they have demonstrated they have leadership traits.

- It is only natural for conflict to happen when people from different backgrounds work together. Expect conflict to emerge, and manage it before eruptions occur.

- Acknowledge differences and be prepared to meet in the middle.

- Be an employee, not a parent, if you want your manager to act like a boss instead of like your child.

- Help your boss feel comfortable. Ask for advice so he knows you recognize he is in charge. If you have little interest in your manager's position, let him know so he sees you as an ally, rather than a predator. Seek his assistance if you are interested in working toward a promotion.

- Make your boss successful. If she is successful, you'll be successful.

- Good leadership skills have nothing to do with age. Be open to the possibility that this person may be the best manager you'll ever have.

*Early in my career, I was hired to replace someone who was being promoted. She couldn't take on her new job until she had trained me. In her new role, this person was responsible for also overseeing my work. I was told I had to do the work her way and couldn't deviate in the smallest way even if the work product was good. It took me quite a while to figure out that she might have feared that someone could actually fit into her shoes. She was struggling with how to move on to her new pasture. She was a person who didn't like change. She was holding herself back as well because "Martha wasn't trained," even though I was.*

*Don't waste your energy worrying about why the boss is trying to be lousy. They aren't in most cases doing this intentionally. Instead, look at things through the boss's eyes. What need is the boss trying to meet in talking with you that way or asking for things in that manner? Usually he or she is not trying to torment you. Have a conversation privately to let them know how it feels to be treated in that manner. Most people will respond in a positive manner when this situation is brought to his or her attention.*

*You have to listen to your internal voice and see if you can work with this person until you figure out what you need to do, unless it is an extreme situation where your values tell you this isn't a place where you can stay.*

Martha S. LaCroix, SPHR
*Chief Human Resources Officer*
*Shane Co.*

## CHAPTER FIVE

# Dealing with a Bad Boss

## There's One in Every Crowd

**H**ave you ever dreamed about giving your boss a one-way ticket to a remote island, similar to the destinations for the reality television show *Survivor*? If so, you are not alone. I personally know few people who haven't had the experience of working for a bad boss. Even presidents of large corporations are saddled from time to time with bad bosses.

Recently, Steve Tobak of BNET.com interviewed Joel Manby, CEO of Herschend Family Entertainment, a privately held $300 million company with 10,000 employees and twenty-four theme parks around the country. Manby shared his thoughts on working in a culture of intimidation and a life-changing moment that he experienced while working as president and CEO of Saab USA.

"I don't want to bash GM, but [intimidation] was part of the culture there. You would get ridiculed in meetings. The CEOs had big egos and had no problem making you look silly," states Manby. He shares the story of a time when he was summoned to Europe by the president of all of Saab. He received a call on a Sunday morning and was on a plane to Europe that day. Upon arrival, he was chewed out for four hours and then got back on a plane to return home. He recalls feeling so humiliated. "That's when I began looking at other opportunities," he stated.

You, too, may eventually decide that the environment you are in is no longer a place you can stay. But in the meantime, if you have a lousy boss, you'll need to learn how to deal with him, so you don't wind up taking his terror out on your own employees and your family.

# Different Versions of the Same Theme

Bad bosses come in different packages. I'm listing some of the more popular varieties, along with tips on how to manage these situations.

### "GO LEFT, NO, GO RIGHT": DEALING WITH AN INDECISIVE BOSS

These are the bosses who tell you to do one thing, then question why the heck you are going in the direction they ordered you to go. Maddening? Yes. However, there are ways you can minimize the number of times this happens.

I have found that with these types of bosses, it's best to confirm what is being asked of you before you proceed. Here's what such a confirmation might sound like: "So, Doug, if I understand you correctly, you would like me to look into moving the customer service call center to Portland, Maine, right? And you would like my recommendations on your desk, along with the supporting documentation, no later than April first. Is that correct?" Follow this conversation with a memo confirming what is being asked and letting your boss know you will get right on it. The last thing you need, after making the call center move, is to find that your boss meant Portland, Oregon. This approach of explicit confirmation will cement what has been agreed upon and will minimize the indecisiveness that is common with bosses like this.

### "I'VE GOT YOU UNDER MY THUMB" BOSSES

Oh, those micromanagers. They'd like you to believe they are managing every detail because they consider themselves to be perfectionists. However, in most cases, the real story is about lack of trust. Think about a time when you may have done some micromanaging. Most likely this occurred when you didn't trust that others would do as good a job as you could.

Micromanagers need to be closely managed, which is ironic if you think about it. The idea here is to build trust. You accomplish this by consistently doing what you say you will do. If you are working for a boss like this, then I suggest you do the following. Think about why it would be in the best interest of your boss to allow you to work more independently. Most likely it will allow him more time to focus on other tasks or will free up time he can spend with family or friends. Once you have established this, you can make a request for more autonomy. Here's how your suggestion might sound: "I am wondering if you would consider allowing me to provide you with a weekly update on the specific project we are working on rather than the daily follow-up that is currently occurring. This approach will give you more time to focus on bringing in new business and making it home in time for dinner with your new wife. I will be sure to keep you informed of anything that might get in the way of us meeting our deadlines, prior to our weekly meeting. How does that sound?" Good, now take out your calendar and set aside time for your weekly meetings.

## BOSSES WHO PLAY FAVORITES

If you've ever worked for a boss like this or your current boss appears to have a favorite, you know how frustrating this can be. It seems like no matter how great a job you do, the boss's pet will do better. Here lies the problem. You have to stop comparing yourself to others in your boss's domain, as you are unlikely to become the favored one by doing so. As my mentor, Alan Weiss, always says, "If you want to be loved, get a dog."

The best way to get others to recognize your contributions is to consistently do good work. You also need to toot your own horn so others can hear your music, which will be discussed in more detail in chapter 6. If you do this, in time you will receive the recognition you deserve. However, if favoritism continues to be a problem, you may want to consider having a conversation with your boss about your observations before you do something as drastic as moving to another job. After all, you have little to lose if you were planning on leaving because of this situation.

Consider that your boss may not realize that she has been favoring others, and may appreciate you bringing this situation to her attention. When having this conversation, stick to the facts you've observed and refrain from bringing in comments others may have made about this situation, as this will likely increase her defensiveness. If your boss's behavior doesn't change, then you have two choices: Live with it or seek a position where the boss treats people more fairly.

## BOSSES WHO DISCRIMINATE

I'd like to tell you that this sort of thing doesn't happen anymore, but I've personally experienced it and have heard from others this is still happening in the workplace. When you are in these situations, your first reaction may be disbelief. Then comes denial and, for most people, anger.

When I worked for a financial consulting firm, I recall my peers noticing that I was being treated differently than they were. They asked, more than one time, if I thought it had to do with the fact that I was a different religion from 95 percent of the people in the firm, including my boss. I brushed off their comments as if they were crazy. In retrospect, I was in denial, as this likely was the case.

Of course, there are laws against workplace discrimination that safeguard a number of protected classes, including religion. I made the decision not to avail myself of these protections, as I preferred to use my energy to find a workplace that valued diversity. Your situation may be very different, and the legal route is certainly one way to put a stop to this. But, even if you win a discrimination case, you have to ask yourself whether this is really the type of organization you want to work for.

Age discrimination seems to be a very hot topic today, as workers fight to avoid extinction. Age discrimination is real. There, I said it. And whoever tells you that it doesn't exist needs a new pair of glasses. But there are ways to minimize this. Here are a few:

- **Stay relevant**—Technology is changing the way work gets done. If you don't know what a tweet is or if WordPerfect is your word processing software of choice, then you have some work to do. Sign up for an online class (you do know what those are, don't you?) or hire a college student to introduce you to the world of social media. Attend seminars and workshops so that you are continuously learning.

- **Look relevant**—Okay, here's the part where people usually go a little crazy on me. First impressions count. Admit it. You too pass judgment the first time you see someone who looks different from everyone else. If you are a woman, update your hairstyle and throw out any clothing with shoulder pads. Men would benefit from investing in some business casual clothes that don't have a label that says "Dockers" on the back of them. Investing in a few new ties for those occasions when you may need them isn't a bad idea either.

- **Listen more than you talk**—So much can be learned about current trends just by listening to what younger people are talking about. I recall walking into the office of a prospect who worked in the advertising industry and commenting immediately on the Jonas Brothers posters hanging in the conference room. He was impressed that I knew who they were. I smiled and then went home and thanked my then eight-year-old daughter for having the Disney Channel on 24/7!

## THE SCREAMER

There are two different kinds of screamers. One is the boss who screams *for* you, even though your office is next door to hers. Even worse, as Janyce Brandon, currently business manager at VITAHL Medical Aesthetics of Cherry Creek, Colorado can attest, is the boss who yells orders via an intermediary: "I once had a boss who would tell my manager to let me know to work on a project despite the fact that my office door was ten feet away and I could hear him. One time he even yelled it down the stairs to my manager, and my office was literally next to the stairs. To get around this, I started catching him on his breaks to make him explain his projects, and he learned to speak directly to me instead of the passive tactic he previously used."

The other kind of screamer is the one who yells *at* employees, and often does so in front of other employees. You have to take this person head on, unless of course you enjoy being in an abusive situation. As I tell my coaching clients, no one deserves to be in a relationship where he is being abused and this is certainly one form of abuse. I'm not suggesting that you yell back, as this will only escalate the volume. Instead, I am recommending that you let this person know you will no longer stand there as he verbally abuses you. In private, tell the offender you are more apt to hear what he is saying if he speaks to you, rather than yells at you. Then be prepared to walk away the next time he reams you out in front of others, as this is one habit that is hard to break.

## THE WORKAHOLIC

This is the boss who believes that, because she has no life, no one else deserves to have a life. She expects you to work evenings, weekends, and, in some cases, holidays. The best way to deal with a workaholic is to manage the expectations upfront. When you begin your job, arrive and depart during normal office hours. Turn your mobile device off in the evenings and on weekends, so your boss doesn't get accustomed to being able to reach you after hours. Resist the temptation to respond to his or her e-mails on weekends, or this will become the new norm.

If you are already in this type of situation, I suggest that you pull back slowly. Begin by scaling back on your "home office" hours. Then work on leaving the office a bit earlier. Get yourself an outside life, so you have reasons to leave at a normal hour.

# Choosing Your Weapon Carefully— Strategies to Help You Survive a Bad Boss

There will be times in your career when you won't be able to walk into your boss's office and quit because of economic conditions or family obligations. The weapon you choose to deal with these types of bosses will depend on your tolerance level, your employability, and the general job market. Here are some strategies that have helped me and others I know survive during tumultuous times.

**Fly below the radar screen**—Have you ever noticed that the kids who keep to themselves often avoid getting picked on in the schoolyard? The same holds true in the workplace. If you can manage to keep your head down and do your job (in spite of what is going on around you), you may be able to survive this boss until you either find a new job or your boss is promoted or terminated.

**Ignore**—Sometimes the best action is inaction. I have found that when employees refuse to acknowledge bullying bosses, those bosses turn their attention to others.

**Pray**—There is nothing wrong with prayer and meditation to get you through these types of situations. I spent many evenings meditating after a hard day at work with one of the lousiest bosses I've ever encountered. Eventually, I decided that I preferred to spend my evenings taking salsa lessons. That was when I decided it was my time to find a job where meditation was a choice, not a requirement to get through my days.

**Meet the boss head on**—If you've got a bad boss, a bully grown up, then you may be best off meeting this person head on. You have to stand up for your rights and for those of the people you manage. Failing to do so will result in the strengthening of this monster, making it extremely difficult to fend this person off.

## What to Do When All Else Fails

Managers have only two options available to them when it comes to working with a bad boss: Deal with it or leave. Some of you may think you have a third choice—hanging in the "contamination zone." This is where you'll find people moaning and groaning about whatever is ailing them, in this case usually the boss. When you are in this zone, it's virtually impossible to keep your feelings about your boss a secret. This means you can quickly taint the people who report to you. That's why it's important early on to decide whether you are going to deal with it or remove yourself from the situation.

Remember that there is power in numbers. You stand a better chance of ousting a bad boss if there are others in the organization who also feel abused or mismanaged. You will have to quietly gather your allies before approaching the person in charge of your boss or the board of directors. You will also need to come armed with evidence on how this is affecting productivity and, most importantly, profitability. You'll need to feel very confident that something will be done, as there is a good chance your boss could declare war and you will most likely be the first one shot.

If you've reviewed many of the suggestions offered in this chapter and none of them feels right for you, then you know what you have to do. Just be sure to read chapter 9, "Seven Signs Your Time Is Up," before resigning, to ensure you know exactly what to ask for on the way out.

## How to Avoid Following in Your Bad Boss's Footsteps

Why do you think there are so many bad bosses out there? Most likely, it's because we learn from what we see. Rory Rowland of Rowland Consulting interviewed approximately 200 people for his book *My Best Boss Ever* and found that only about a third of the people he spoke with had experienced a great boss. Most rated their bosses as mediocre or poor. Think about it. You work for a boss who's a jerk. You observe everything about him, rather than about his employees. Yet he's the guy driving the BMW, which he parks in a space reserved for him, while you ride the bus to work every day. You put two and two together and conclude that in order to achieve success like your boss, you have to act like your boss. And so the cycle continues. That is, it continues until you are lucky enough to work for an outstanding boss, one who demonstrates that it is possible to be a leader who is well respected, admired, *and* successful.

There are lots of ways to get to the same place. But at the end of the day, you have to live with yourself. Even in today's sophisticated business climate, we see abusive bosses who manage to thrive in organizations in spite of, or perhaps because of, their abrasive management style. As a new generation takes over the leadership of firms, the values and beliefs of the workplace will shift. An abusive management style may no longer yield the same results. Most of you who are reading this book have just stepped into management. You have an opportunity to create a management revolution—it will be up to you to craft a work environment where lousy bosses need not apply. Like any revolution, the change must start with you.

## LESSONS LEARNED FROM BAD BOSSES: HOW *NOT* TO MANAGE

Most of us have experienced or will experience what it is like to work for someone who falls far short of what we would consider an effective leader. Here are some stories from the trenches and lessons learned along the way.

1.  Vanessa Jackson, principal of Matrix Human Resource Solutions, worked for a boss who liked to belittle people in front of their colleagues. She shared the following story with me. "I had to give a presentation for a group of mid-level staff managers (such as myself) and mispronounced the name of our company's auditors. My boss made fun of my mispronunciation in front of my colleagues and told me if I could not say the name correctly then there was no need for me to say it at all (meaning I would not facilitate further presentations, even though I had developed the presentation)." Vanessa learned two things from this experience: Anyone can get a little tongue-tied when she is under pressure and to "praise in public and give feedback/constructive criticism in private!"

2.  Bosses who are self-centered seem to create memorable experiences for their workers, for the wrong reasons. This is exemplified

by a boss who, at performance review time, said, "You surpassed every goal, but I'm not giving you your bonus because it will impact mine." Anecdote courtesy of Linda Konsta, president of LMK Associates/Sensible Human Resources Consulting.

3. Keep in mind that your success (and bonus) will be directly affected by your ability to achieve the goals for your management group. It will be very difficult, if not impossible, to do so if most of what you do is about you and not about helping your employees succeed.

4. Harriet Cohen, owner of Training Solutions, returned to her consulting firm after a two-year stint as a director for a company where she reported to the CEO and COO. Cohen provided me with a laundry list of poor management practices that she observed during her time with this company. One in particular caught my attention: "When I first started, my boss would ask if she could give me feedback, then she would ream me, asking, 'What were you thinking? I know you weren't thinking.' After a few times, I got smart and said no thank you to the feedback." Cohen added, "I'm in a very good place right now, while she is still making people miserable."

---

## KEY LEARNING POINTS

- Bad bosses come in a variety of flavors. Some are easier to digest than others. To keep your stomach from churning, you have to decide how you will deal with the situation or you have to remove yourself. Your decision about whether to stay or go will determine your course of action.

- Indecisiveness is not a trait highly valued in management. If you happen to have a boss with this syndrome, you will need to modify the way you manage this person. Always clarify what your boss is asking for and follow up in writing to ensure you are in agreement.

- Micromanagement is not about perfection; it is about lack of trust. The best way to manage a boss like this is to build trust. Do this by delivering what you promise and by identifying for your boss why it's in her best interest to provide you with more autonomy.

- Discrimination in the workplace is real. If you are facing discrimination, determine your best course of action, which in many cases may not involve attorneys.

- There are many strategies you can employ to help you cope with a bad boss while figuring out your next move. Strategies include flying below the radar screen, ignoring the situation, prayer and meditation, and taking the boss head on.
- When all else fails, you have the choice of bringing your concerns to those higher up in the organization—unless, of course, your boss *is* the organization.
- You are the next generation of managers. You have the power to start a management revolution, and to create work environments where lousy bosses are no longer tolerated.

---

*I'm Canadian and female. This concept of tooting your own horn was uncomfortable to me. I used to think if I kept on doing a really, really great job, people would notice. Women are particularly guilty of this. When people don't notice, you are surprised and you ask yourself, "How did they not notice?"*

*Earlier in my career, I worked in a relatively large company where all the top executive salaries were made public. I was one of those executives—they were my peers and I was making half of what they were making in some cases.*

*I realized I had outsourced the responsibility to manage my compensation to the company. It was at that moment that I understood I would need to take matters into my own hands. I went to my boss and said, "This isn't going to work. Explain this to me. You are going to have to fix this." And he did.*

*Think of yourself as your own product. You are responsible for promoting yourself. It's your responsibility to get yourself noticed and to get compensated for what you are worth.*

*Stepping up to take on problems that need to be solved is a great way to stand out. That's what leaders do. They also focus on results, rather than activities.*

Christy Wyatt
*CEO*
*Dtex Systems*

## CHAPTER SIX

# Tooting Your Own Horn

## So You Can Be Heard in a Sea of Cubicles

In today's workplace, there is so much competition for attention that it may feel impossible to stand out and get noticed. So what can a new manager do to be heard above a sea of cubicles? You have to forget everything your mother ever taught you about not bragging! Pump up the volume and make enough noise so people in the organization know who you are and are aware of what you are accomplishing. You don't want to be obnoxious in promoting yourself, but others in the organization need to know your value, and they're not likely to find out unless you make them aware.

Given the constant changes in corporate life—buyouts, downsizing, office closings—you simply must excel at keeping more than just your boss informed of your successes, as there is no guarantee she will be there tomorrow. This can be particularly challenging today, as executives are bombarded with text, e-mail, and voicemail messages, together with a full schedule of meetings, which leaves them little time to focus on you. That's why you have to give them a reason to stop and pay attention. We'll go into detail about how you can make this happen after we discuss why it will take more than one strong performance to separate yourself from the crowd.

## Why Your Performance Alone
## Won't Take You to the Top

The hit show *American Idol*, which ran from 2002 to 2016, is a good example of how performance alone may not take you to the top. In this show, singers performed in front of judges and a television audience, competing to be the next breakthrough star. What made this competition so interesting is that often the runner-up, or a finalist in the top ten, went on to have a more successful career than the person crowned the winner. I believe much of this is due to how well the participants leveraged their brand after the season ended.

Here's an example. Can you guess the season three winner of *American Idol* from the following choices?

- John Stevens
- Fantasia Barrino
- Jennifer Hudson
- Jasmine Trias

The correct answer depends on how you define "winner." While Fantasia Barrino was the official winner of *American Idol*, many might argue that the real winner was Jennifer Hudson. And she has the Oscar to prove it. If you've ever heard Hudson sing, you know she has no problems being heard.

Now think of colleagues or people you know who have done great work, yet never made it to the top of their profession. At the same time, you can probably list a number of average or even poor performers who seemed to get promoted in spite of themselves. These people have built a fan base, and I can guarantee it didn't happen without some noisemaking.

## Playing in Harmony

Have you ever noticed how the sounds of the quieter instruments in the orchestra resonate, even after the performance is over? My ears perk up when I hear the sweet sounds of the piccolo playing gently in the background, whereas I usually tune out the louder instruments, like the tuba.

As Dan Bowling points out, sometimes the best way to get noticed is to sit quietly in the background while those around you take center stage. Of course, as a manager you have to make sure you orchestrate this move so your people have a platform where they can shine. Allowing your direct reports to be heard and recognized is one of the most effective ways to toot your own horn as a manager. If you do this consistently, others will begin to notice that your people seem always to be playing in harmony. You will be recognized as a strong leader who can motivate her people to perform beautifully and can change tunes at the drop of a hat.

## Some Common Myths about Self-Promotion

The sooner you bust through these common myths about self-promotion, the quicker you will be noticed.

### MYTH #1: YOUR WORK SPEAKS FOR ITSELF

If all you needed to get noticed was great work, why is it that so many great artists never became famous until they died? Your work is just your work, until someone takes notice. If you want it to be in this lifetime, then you will have to attract attention. We'll discuss exactly how to do that in this chapter.

### MYTH #2: YOU DON'T HAVE TO BRAG BECAUSE OTHER PEOPLE WILL DO IT FOR YOU

I know lots of people who are still waiting around for someone to recognize them for work they completed months and in some cases years ago. I suspect they are waiting at the dock for a ship that will never come in. You have to take charge of your own publicity campaign. In her book *Brag! The Art of Tooting Your Own Horn without Blowing It*, author Peggy Klaus writes, "No one is going to have your interests at heart the way you do. No one will ever tell your story and get people excited about you like you can. Plus, nine times out of ten, when those to whom you report talk positively about your work to others, it's usually because there is something in it for them. Unfortunately, the accolade is framed in such a way as to bolster them, more than you!"

I couldn't agree more with Klaus. I've always told my own stories and have never relied on anyone to do so on my behalf. I may not get every word right, but I certainly make up for it by the way I deliver my messages.

## MYTH #3: PATTING YOURSELF ON THE BACK IS ONLY APPROPRIATE DURING PERFORMANCE REVIEW TIME

Many people put together a list of their accomplishments only at review time. This may occur because nothing outstanding appears to be happening throughout the year. The key word here is *appears*, as most likely you are making huge strides as you knock off goal after goal. The unfortunate thing is that you (and perhaps a loved one) are the only ones who know about it.

Most layoffs don't fall conveniently at review time. If the last great thing your boss knows about happened nine months ago, you may be chopped before you've had an opportunity to present your accomplishments. Self-promotion year-round is necessary, so you remain one of "the keepers" all year long.

## MYTH #4: IT'S NOT LADYLIKE TO BRAG

Women have been conditioned to believe that it's poor manners to brag. So for years, they have stood back while their male counterparts shared their success stories with anyone who would listen. Today, women are competing at the same level as men, and, therefore, it is necessary to play by the same rules, which include letting others in the organization know what a valuable resource you are to the firm.

## MYTH #5: HUMBLENESS IS A VALUED TRAIT

As children, we learn the importance of being humble. We are taught not to brag about our family's financial status or to gloat about all the trophies or medals we've acquired in sport-related activities. Being understated may be fine when you are a child, but will it get you ahead as an adult? In most situations, the answer is no. Why? Because while you are being humble, others are banging the drum loudly regarding their latest accomplishments. You fade into the background, while they take center stage.

## MYTH #6: PEOPLE WON'T LIKE YOU IF YOU BRAG

I recently rode home from New York City with a colleague. During our three-and-a-half-hour drive, I learned a great deal about her that made me like her even more than I had before we'd taken that drive. She had accomplished so much in her career, yet had never shared this information with me or with her prospects. She had taken risks that few of us would have been brave enough to try, and she had some funny stories to prove it. If she didn't toot her own horn while driving home, I would not have discovered this part of her personality.

Think about those accomplishments you may never have shared with others. How would others perceive you if you showed them a part of you that you've withheld for years? Would you be considered more of a risk taker? Would they have more respect for you? Would you perhaps be viewed as a viable candidate for an overseas assignment? Imagine all the possibilities that might unfold if you simply let people know why you are unique.

# Bad Bragging versus Good Bragging (There Is a Difference)

The Merriam-Webster dictionary defines the verb "brag" as "to talk boastfully." Is this really the type of behavior we want to embrace?

In an interview by Shari Lifland of the American Management Association, Peggy Klaus, author of *Brag! The Art of Tooting Your Own Horn without Blowing It*, does an outstanding job of differentiating between bad and good bragging. Klaus notes that if "we all acted like big blowhards, our clients and coworkers would make a mad dash for the door. That kind of behavior is bad bragging. Good bragging is completely different; it's highlighting a few memorable tidbits of information about yourself in an interesting and entertaining story expressed with passion and delight."

Here are three common bragging mistakes found in the work-place:

1. **Bad timing**—Don't brag about the new overseas assignment you've received when your colleague has been transferred to the least desirable location imaginable. You never know. This person could one day be your boss, and may choose to get even.

2. **Insensitivity to priorities**—Wait to brag to your boss until she is relaxed and you have her full attention. Updating your boss after she has spent the weekend completing a huge project is a big mistake—if all she can think about is going home to get some sleep yet you insist on taking this moment to fill her in on all your accomplishments, how do you think the scenario will play out? I'm guessing not well.

3. **Too many potatoes and not enough meat**—Don't tell the boss about *everything* you do; reserve your bragging for the juicy stuff. If you overinform, your boss will eventually tune you out, as she searches for a reason to take this conversation off her plate.

## Becoming a Person of Interest

I often hear people say they would have no problems promoting themselves if only they had something worth promoting. Most of us have plenty to brag about, we just may need some help to bring these ideas to the forefront of our brains.

Here are some questions you can ask yourself to get your brain waves moving in the right direction. Refer to the sidebar on page 72 for more questions to spur self-promotion.

1. What three things have you done in your life that you are extremely proud of? (Hint: Have you traveled extensively? Have you done volunteer work? Did you pay for your own schooling? Have you applied for a patent? Did you achieve a milestone in your career before most of your peers? Have you made a difference in someone's life?)

2. What have you accomplished that you haven't readily shared with others?

3. What are three things you would say about yourself that demonstrate the value you bring to the organization? What are three things your colleagues would name about your contributions?

4. What projects have you worked on in the past (or you are currently working on) that showcase your talent?

5. What awards have you received both in and outside the workplace?

6. What are some of your aspirations? (Hint: Are you attending graduate school? Are you participating in a local theater group? Are you learning to speak a foreign language?)

7.  What do you think is your strongest asset, and how might you continue to fine-tune your skills?

# Five Ways to Toot Your Horn So Your Work Is Noticed

Let's talk about ways to make certain your work is noticed, now that you have a better sense of why it's in your best interest to master the art of Strategic Bragging™ and you've taken the time to determine your unique value proposition.

1.  **Storytelling**—Everyone loves a story, particularly a good story. Think about how you can weave what you'd like to brag about into a story. For example, when I completed my MBA, I quit my job and traveled around the world by myself for an entire year. I had some amazing experiences along the way. There, I just used Strategic Bragging™ to tell you about three things in my life without boasting. You now know I have an MBA, that I'm a world traveler who has experienced many cultures firsthand, and that I'm a risk taker. But my presentation is much more interesting than if I had simply listed those three items.

    I told this story when I was applying for a position as a director of human resources in an organization with a very diverse workforce. The hiring manager, who eventually became my boss, was impressed that I was able to relate easily to people of different nationalities, and that it was likely I had spent time in their country at some point in my travels. He also perceived me as a risk taker and a real go-getter, which were traits highly valued in the organization.

2.  **Deliver with confidence**—It's all about the delivery. Have you ever noticed how some people look down while they are talking about themselves, or their voice suddenly becomes hard to hear? Conviction and confidence are vital when you are promoting yourself. After all, if you don't believe what you are saying, what makes you think others will?

    This may take some practice. Fortunately, every mobile device these days has the ability to record video. Record yourself as you deliver your story. Then play it back. How well did you project your voice? Did you come across as believable? Did you maintain eye contact when you got to the most boastful part of your story? Keep practicing until your delivery matches the excellence of your story.

3. **Create a master list of boastful moments**—It's hard to remember all those great things you've accomplished, particularly as you get older and add more items to the list. That's why I recommend keeping a list on your computer. This way you can easily retrieve stories when you need them.

   For example, suppose you are going to be driving to a conference with your boss and the vice president of your division. What would you like the VP to know about you that she may not be aware of? Is there something you can throw into the conversation naturally that would put you in a good light? If the conference you are attending is on the use of social media, for instance, do you have examples of how you have successfully used social media to build community? Perhaps you have done this with your son's scout group. Or maybe you have been an expert blogger for a well-known website like Fast Company. This certainly would be of interest, given the topic of the conference. And who knows, after the conference the VP may invite you to participate on the highly visible task force she is assembling to leverage social media and build profitability.

4. **Lead, don't just follow**—Many people join associations, yet few get involved. Here you have an opportunity to shine within your industry, which will get you noticed by more than just your boss. Identify one organization and make a commitment to do more than show up for the monthly meetings. Become active on committees like membership or get involved in programs that offer high visibility. As a long-term goal, consider becoming the president, which will really get you noticed!

5. **Volunteer for highly visible projects within your own organization**—Let's face it. In just about every organization, the CEO has a cause that he or she volunteers employees to join. In your company it may be United Way, or perhaps it's a walk to stamp out hunger. Someone is going to be assigned to lead this cause, so why not make sure that someone is you? This will give you direct access to the corner office and allow you to demonstrate that you are capable of leading a high-profile initiative. Of course, it doesn't hurt that this campaign is near and dear to the heart of the person who ultimately controls how far you will go in the organization.

   Another way to make yourself stand out in the crowd is to seek out opportunities to join company initiatives that require representatives from a number of departments. Remember, visibility is the name of the game. We talked earlier about why it's important to get the attention of those other than your boss, particularly when the economy is a bit shaky. Volunteer to be the liaison between the team and management so you have the opportunity to present your findings to those higher up in the organization.

6. **Keep your boss updated on your accomplishments**—The key here is to figure out your boss's communication preferences and to use this information to share your accomplishments. If you have a boss who prefers monthly reports, then at the end of the month send him a tally of progress under your direction. Be sure to avoid bombarding your manager with snippets of self-promotion; otherwise, your memos will soon be deleted before they are even read. Here is where being succinct comes into play. Tell your boss what you have to say and nothing more. If more information is needed, you will be asked to provide it.

You'll know you've mastered the art of tooting your own horn when your boss applauds your efforts and asks you to share more.

## SAGE ADVICE FROM EXPERT STORYTELLER SALLY STRACKBEIN

Mention the word "brag" to most people and watch them shrink back in horror. Common bragging is something only obnoxious, self-centered people do. But how do you get ahead if no one knows about your accomplishments? Unlike the common brag, Strategic Bragging™ is the art of telling your success stories so that people say, "Tell me more." No one wants to hear, "Yay me. I'm great. Look at me!" But everyone wants to hear a good story with a happy ending. It's all in how you weave your tale. An interesting brag story begins with a bit of scene setting, just like in the movies. Do this in only a sentence or two. Then explain what problem you solved, how you solved it, and the results you got. The key is to listen to other people first, and when they ask about you, say, "For example," and tell your story.

## BRAG! TAKE THE SELF-EVALUATION QUESTIONNAIRE

Author Peggy Klaus offers valuable questions designed to get you promoting yourself effectively in her book *BRAG! The Art of Tooting Your Own Horn without Blowing It* (2003). Don't feel that you have to answer these questions in order. You can start anywhere and skip around. As you move through the questions, you'll likely think of things you might have overlooked when answering earlier ones. In fact, you'll probably want to go over your responses again after you have completed the evaluation. Remember, the more time you put into this exercise, and the more specific details you provide, the easier it will be to create brag bites and bragologues that will be crystal clear and interesting to those who don't already know you well.

1.  What would you and others say are five of your personality pluses?
2.  What are the ten most interesting things you have done or that have happened to you?
3.  What do you do for a living and how did you end up doing it?
4.  What do you like/love about your current job/career?
5.  How does your job/career use your skills and talents, and what projects are you working on right now that best showcase them?
6.  What career successes are you most proud of having accomplished (from current position and past jobs)?
7.  What new skills have you learned in the last year?
8.  What obstacles have you overcome to get where you are today, both professionally and personally, and what essential lessons have you learned from some of your mistakes?
9.  What training/education have you completed and what did you gain from those experiences?
10. What professional organizations are you associated with and in what ways—member, board, treasurer, or the like?
11. How do you spend your time outside of work, including hobbies, interests, sports, family, and volunteer activities?
12. In what ways are you making a difference in people's lives?

-------------------- KEY LEARNING POINTS --------------------

- When trying to get noticed, first and foremost you have to be authentic. If you are not, you'll be uncomfortable doing so and will most likely stop, which will affect your ability to gain the resources needed to continue to support both your people and yourself.

- Pump up the volume! Forget about what you've learned at home or what others have told you about bragging. You have to make enough noise so people in the organization take notice of who you are and what you are able to accomplish.

- Your performance alone won't take you to the top. You may be the best singer in the room, but no one will know this if you never open your mouth.

- Showcase your people. When they look good, you look fantastic!

- Myths about self-promotion are just that—myths. No one ever got ahead or obtained more resources for their people by following a set of rules that no longer make sense in today's workplace. Take ownership for your own PR by letting others know about your work and the work of your people, and do so all year long. If anyone has a problem with this, be sure to loan him this book!

- Ladies (and I do mean ladies), your mother was wrong. Women have been conditioned to believe that it is not ladylike to brag. I say brag away if you want to play on the same field as your male counterparts.

- Timing is everything. Take stock of what is going on around you before sharing your latest victory. The last thing you want to do is trumpet great news when those around you appear to be having a tough day.

- Unfortunately, Storytelling 101 is not usually offered at most universities. That means you are going to have to fine-tune this skill on your own. The Brag! Take the Self-Evaluation Questionnaire sidebar will help get you started.

*Executive presence matters more than many people realize. When I hear the words* executive presence, *I think of the four P's: Professional, Put together, Polished, and Poised. This powerful combination allows leaders to set themselves apart from the pack.*

*I'm moving someone out of a role because he doesn't command executive presence. I promoted a very high performer into a senior level role, and when we are in the room together, he's invisible. He's quiet, submissive, and has not stepped up, even after working with a coach.*

*If you take one of these roles, people must know you are in the room. You have to be interested and interesting! When you step up and take the role of a leader, you have to make sure you are ready for that.*

Joyce Russell
*President*
*Adecco Staffing US*

## CHAPTER SEVEN

# Executive Presence: There's More to Executive Presence than Looks

Quick, what comes to mind when you hear the words *executive presence*? Jot down your response. I've conducted executive presence workshops for a number of companies, including Microsoft, and I have opened the session with this exercise. I'm always surprised by how many different words come up to describe the same thing. To ensure that we are on the same page, here's my definition.

> Executive presence is the aura of leadership. It's that feeling people get when a leader walks in the room.

Executive presence is not about wearing an expensive suit, although dress does matter. Nor is it about having a firm handshake or simply surrounding yourself with the right people. Rather, it's about the way you make people feel when they are in your presence.

When it comes to executive presence, keep in mind that actions speak louder than words. Make sure you take the time to think through everything you do and how those around you may perceive it. Sure, you'll make some mistakes. Everyone does. But it's what you do with these mistakes that matters most. If you can learn to adjust your style as needed, it won't be long before people say, "She just gets it."

# How to Develop Executive Presence

Before we move on, let's take a more detailed look at the specific elements required to develop your executive presence.

## PROJECT CONFIDENCE

Former President Obama has executive presence. So does Jamaican sprinter Usain Bolt, tennis great Serena Williams, and former GE CEO Jack Welch. No man or woman attains a top job or position without confidence. When these people walk into the room, you have no doubt they know they belong there.

Think about a leader for whom you have high levels of respect. This person could be your boss or someone else. What do you notice when this person walks into a meeting? Most likely she enters the room as if she owns it. She takes her place at the table, while others scramble to sit by her side. You have no doubt who is running this show. Successful people believe in their skills and talent.

Now think about your own situation. How would you rate yourself when it comes to confidence? You have a choice. You can wake up every day and charge into work with optimism, or you can slog your way through the day wondering when people are going to figure out you don't belong here. I hope you'll choose optimism.

In leadership expert Marshall Goldsmith's book *What Got You Here Won't Get You There*,[1] Goldsmith talks about self-efficacy, which he believes may be the most central belief driving individual success. "People who believe they can succeed see opportunities where others see threats," notes Goldsmith. "They're not afraid of uncertainty or ambiguity. They embrace it. Given the choice, they will always bet on themselves."

I want you to think about this the next time you find yourself challenged by an assignment. I hope you will bet on yourself. Better yet, double down.

## BE POISED UNDER PRESSURE

Imagine being a professional baseball player. It's the last inning, bases are loaded, there are two outs, and you're at bat. Your team is trailing

---

[1] Marshall Goldsmith, *What Got You Here Won't Get You There* (New York: Hyperion, 2007), p. 20.

by two runs. You step up to the plate and you take a stand. Pros like retired Boston Red Sox player David Ortiz have prepared their entire lives for this moment. Imagine if Ortiz stood there and thought, "Gee, I'm not sure I can do this. The pressure is killing me." Instead, he learned to manage the pressure and to use it to his advantage. You can do the same.

The best way to prepare yourself to handle pressure with poise is to think through every scenario that may occur and practice your response. For example, suppose you've been asked to present the new customer retention strategy your team has been working on to the executive committee. There are a limited number of questions they may ask. Think about what these are and prepare a response. Keep in mind you are the expert on this strategy because you've designed it.

## DEMONSTRATE DECISIVENESS

Leaders are given authority and are expected to use it. People gravitate to leaders who are decisive. Imagine for a moment you are meeting with the CEO and his executive team. The CEO says, "I'm thinking we should acquire this company, although I'm not 100 percent convinced this is the best strategy." He'd be thrown out of the boardroom before he could say the word *convinced*.

One of the biggest complaints I hear from employees is that their manager can't make a decision. Can't or won't? If I'm going to follow a leader, I sure as heck want to know she knows exactly where she is going. Your people expect you to be decisive, and so does your manager. Making decisions is one of the riskiest parts of a manager's job, but it's also one of the most important. Effective leaders gather the facts, examine the alternatives, and choose the best course possible, given what they know—and they do it quickly. They certainly don't stand around twiddling their thumbs and vacillating back and forth.

Moreover, once a decision is made, they don't second-guess their actions. They move at lightning speed. Rarely is a decision perfect. That's why effective leaders are masters at adjusting course while moving forward. Some decision is better than no decision. If you make a mistake, fix it.

## COMMUNICATE EFFECTIVELY

Executives with executive presence have this uncanny ability to transform us with their language. My client Catherine D'Amato, CEO of the Greater Boston Food Bank, is one such leader. When D'Amato speaks, people listen. Her ability to draw people into her vision and to support the mission of the organization is uncanny. I believe this is so because she is always authentic. Some CEOs never express doubt, nor do they admit that every decision they have made may not have been the right decision. D'Amato readily shares her mistakes with her team members and is the first to admit when she is wrong.

Take a look at your own communication style. When you speak, do others listen or do they pick up their phones to check their texts? Communication skills can be learned. If you feel yours could benefit from some pizzazz, consider hiring a coach to help you present yourself in a way that is compelling.

### READ AN AUDIENCE OR A SITUATION

I once worked for a boss who was a master at reading the audience or any situation that was in front of him. This trait was the reason why he was an incredibly successful salesperson. He'd walk into the room, quickly scan the audience, and determine if the group was friendly. If they were not, he'd say something that disarmed them. Needless to say, he was quite likeable.

The ability to read a room comes with practice and experience. Take a look at people in your organization who do this well. Ask them to share some of their tips with you. Then apply these practices until this becomes second nature.

# How to Make a Long-lasting Impression in a Millisecond World

With all the distractions going on in the world, we've got about a millisecond to make a great first impression. This means there is no room for error. Here are some effective tips to help you out.

### DRESS APPROPRIATELY

Does dress matter? You betcha! In many cases today, young workers have rejected formal business attire in exchange for what we now call "business casual." As a result, it's often considered perfectly acceptable to wear jeans and a T-shirt to a meeting with a client. But is it smart? I'll let you decide.

A recent *WSJ* article titled "Why Dressing for Success Leads to Success"[2] highlighted new research that shows that when workers wear nice clothes, they achieve more. According to the article, "Using a number of measures, including simulated business meetings at which subjects wore formal and more casual clothing, the studies offer indications that wearing nicer clothes may raise one's confidence level, affect how others perceive the wearer, and in some cases even boost the level of one's abstract thinking, the type in which leaders and executives engage."

The article highlighted a study cowritten by Michael W. Kraus, an assistant professor of organization behavior at the Yale School of Management, with the *Journal of Experimental Psychology* in 2014, which showed that those who are dressed well can increase dominance and job performance in "high stakes" competitive tasks.[3]

The study put 128 men ages 18 to 32 with diverse backgrounds and income levels through mock negotiations over the sale of a hypothetical factory—to see whether wearing specific kinds of clothing impacted the outcomes. The "buyer" in each case came from one of three groups. One group wore business suits and dress shoes. One group wore sweatpants, white T-shirts, and plastic sandals. A third group, referred to as "neutrals," wore the clothing they arrived in. A neutral played the role of "seller" in each negotiation, but no seller also played a role as a buyer.

The negotiators were each given a fair-market value for the hypothetical factory, along with other information that would influence their decisions about opening bids and asking prices. In the end, the suits proved much less willing to concede ground during the negotiations, moving off their initial offer by an average of only $830,000, compared with $2.81 million for those in sweatpants and $1.58 million for the neutrals.

Here's what I gleaned from this study:

- Wearing nicer clothes may raise your confidence level.
- When you are dressed well, you signal to others that you are successful and are really confident in whatever you're doing.

---

[2] "Why Dressing for Success Leads to Success," Ray A. Smith, *Wall Street Journal*, February 21, 2016.

[3] Michael W. Kraus and Wendy Berry Mendes, "Sartorial Symbols of Social Class Elicit Class-Consistent Behavioral and Physiological Responses: A Dyadic Approach," *Journal of Experimental Psychology* 143, no. 6 (December 2014): 2330–2340. http://psycnet.apa.org/?&fa=main.doiLanding&doi=10.1037/xge0000023.

- Dressing nicely affects how others perceive you.
- In some cases, dressing well boosts the level of your abstract thinking—the type in which leaders and executives routinely engage.
- People see the big picture when they dress more formally. In the study, the casual dressers tended to sweat the small stuff. When you feel more powerful, you don't focus on the details.

I'm not suggesting you have to run out and buy a Brooks Brothers suit. However, you may want to take a closer look at your wardrobe and upgrade some pieces. Women should consider wearing a tailored jacket, especially for an important meeting, and putting on a pair of high-heeled shoes as well. Men may want to keep a tie in their desk in case they find themselves suddenly called into the boardroom.

## BE PRESENT

Step away from your smartphone! I once met an HR executive who was anything but present. She roamed the halls with her smartphone in hand and even had the nerve to text under the table when her boss, who was the CEO, was speaking to her. This woman's addiction to her phone resulted in her demise. It soon became clear that she was not the type of person the CEO wanted representing his organization. She clearly lacked executive presence and was not present!

The leaders I know with executive presence make you feel like you are the only person in the room. They wouldn't dare answer a call when they are in the middle of a conversation with you, nor would they respond to a text.

My advice to you is simple. When speaking to your boss or one of your employees, step away from your phone. Have an uninterrupted conversation, one that is free from distraction. This one small move will have a huge impact on your relationships at work.

## COMMUNICATE WITH AUTHORITY

Either my hearing has worsened over the years or people are speaking more quietly. I find that when managers communicate in meetings, many do so in a soft voice and with little conviction. When having a conversation with your boss or her peers, it's important to come across as confident and well spoken.

It's also important to be aware of world events that may be impacting the business you work for so that you can speak about them with authority. In my experience, few managers read newspapers anymore. Consequently, they seem uninformed. You have an opportunity to easily stand out from the crowd by being well read. I advise my coaching clients to subscribe to the *Wall Street Journal* or the *New York Times* so they can converse intelligently with their manager and other leaders in the organization.

When expressing yourself in a noisy world, it's easy for your message to get drowned out. That's why it's important to be concise and get to the point rapidly. Workers today, including your manager, are time-starved. You've only got a few seconds before they are off to the next thing. Make each second count.

## TAKE CONTROL OF THE ROOM

There are going to be lots of times in your career when you are going to want to have control over the room. You may be presenting a new concept you've been working on for a client pitch to your manager or selling your idea to your boss and the executive team. In these situations, it's important to keep the following in mind.

*Choose your seat wisely.* Plan on arriving early to meetings and mark your territory with a water bottle and your notebook. When possible, take the seat that's next to your boss. Of course, it's also important to mind your manners. While securing a good seat in the room is important, you certainly don't want to dive over one of your coworkers to make it so.

*Increase your eye contact.* Good eye contact engages others. When you fail to make regular eye contact, you miss out on a huge opportunity to connect with your audience.

*Raise your level of confidence.* If you think what you are about to say isn't all that interesting or important, this will change how you present the information. It's important to speak with enthusiasm and conviction, especially when selling an idea to your boss.

*Dial up the volume on your voice.* Your excitement will be contagious!

*Make sure your words match your actions.* It's best to make sure you've done your homework, because once all eyes are upon you, people will expect that you have something worthwhile for them to hear.

# What Holds Many People Back

I've worked with hundreds of leaders as both an adviser and a coach and have found that many struggle with this abstract idea of executive presence. Here's why.

## MINDSET

The biggest impediment to executive presence lies in between your ears. It's called mindset. First and foremost, people refuse to believe that other factors besides performance will be taken into consideration when promotion time comes along. Look around your workplace and see who is being promoted. Are the promotions going to people who are technically great at their jobs, or are other factors coming into play? My guess is it's the latter.

I mentioned earlier that I've conducted workshops on executive presence for some very prestigious organizations. Sometimes these sessions are for women seeking to propel their careers forward. One such session was a clear reminder of how mindset can prevent people from succeeding. A female participant was extremely defensive when we started to discuss how image matters. She could not wrap her head around the idea that while the men in management came to work every day in jeans and a T-shirt and were still seen as authority figures, when she did so, she wasn't taken seriously.

I shared the *WSJ* article *Why Dressing for Success Leads to Success* with the group. In spite of the data and a degree from MIT, she was unable to adjust her thinking. Now keep in mind, I wasn't saying women *needed* to wear skirts and jackets to work in order to be seen as a leader. I was merely sharing the study and suggesting that having a jacket on hand to wear at meetings might help to project a more authoritative image. However, she simply wasn't open to this idea.

## THE IMPOSTOR SYNDROME

Let's say you are in a job that you may not be completely qualified for—at least not yet. You've got this little guy sitting on your shoulders reminding you of this on a daily basis. You keep thinking, When is someone going to figure out that I have no business being in this job?

Earlier we discussed how people with executive presence walk into a room as if they own the room. If, instead, you choose to slip in through the side door with the hopes you won't be noticed, your wish will come true. You won't be noticed. But that's not the outcome we are going for here. Your boss needs to know you can command the room.

You need to get some new self-talk. You have the aptitude to do this job or you wouldn't have been given this assignment. What you don't know, you can quickly learn. Keep telling yourself you deserve to be in this role. Do this daily until you finally believe this.

## SELF-DOUBT

Maybe you keep thinking, "Why would anyone listen to *me*?" Well, with that attitude, they probably won't. This really is a self-esteem issue. If you are going to remain in a leadership role and succeed, you need to exude confidence.

Here's what you should be thinking instead: "I have a lot of value to offer. Who wouldn't want to listen to what I'm about to say?"

# Perfecting Your Presence

Executive presence isn't one of those things you can acquire and then forget about. As you advance in your career, you'll need to up your game. Here are some ideas to help you grow your presence.

**Hone your presentation skills.** The higher up in the organization you go, the more often you'll be asked to present. My advice to you is to start working on this now so you'll feel confident and ready to present at a moment's notice. There are a number of ways to do this, including role-playing with colleagues or with a trusted adviser, joining a local Toastmasters club, speaking at industry association meetings, and presenting at large conferences. Those with more resources may choose to invest in a presentation coach.

**Get rid of bad behaviors.** I was watching a political debate the other day and was taken back with how frequently one candidate was interrupting another. I found his presence annoying. Similar behavior happens in workplaces all the time. Just make sure you're not the one others find off-putting. If you have the tendency to interrupt, count to ten before speaking. This will give you ample opportunity to allow the other person to finish her sentence. Other distracting behavior includes letting your hands do the speaking. It's hard for people to focus on your message when your hands are flying. If need be, put your hands in your pocket.

**Ask your boss, mentor, or coach for help.** If you want your boss to bring you with him to meetings, where you'll gain exposure you won't get elsewhere, pay attention to how you present yourself. Don't be afraid to ask your manager, mentor, or coach for advice on how to improve in this area.

--------------------- KEY LEARNING POINTS ---------------------

- Executive presence is the aura of leadership. It's that feeling people get when a leader walks in the room.
- Those with executive presence project confidence, remain poised under pressure, demonstrate decisiveness, and communicate in a way that gets others to join in with their vision.
- With all the distractions that are going on in the world, we've got about a millisecond to make a great first impression. When it comes to executive presence, dress does matter. Be mindful of your wardrobe choices and update pieces as your budget permits.
- Be present. Step away from your smartphone and fully engage with those who are in your presence.
- Learn to command the room. Choose your seat wisely, pay attention to your manners, and do your homework ahead of time so you can fully contribute to the conversation.
- All leaders have the ability to improve their executive presence. To do so, you need to change your mindset from "I should be judged solely on merit" to "How am I perceived as a leader, and what adjustments do I need to make in order to improve?"
- Leaders who have great executive presence work on maintaining their presence daily. Ask people you respect for feedback, and be willing to try new approaches.

*Mentorship is critical to have. These relationships allow you to ask more questions and learn in a way that is less formal.*

*People get tripped up thinking mentoring has to be a formal ask within an organization. In most situations, someone doesn't say, "I want to be your mentor! I want to show you the ropes."*

*Keep your eyes wide open. When the opportunity to work with a mentor comes around—take it! When you find someone you can relate to, look for ways to get in so you can be in the position of building a relationship that will lead to mentorship. Find ways to add value to that leader so she includes you in different conversations she is having. This will lead to a seat in the balcony and then eventually a seat at the table.*

*There is another side to mentorship that most people don't talk about. When you're a mentor, you have people you've groomed who become part of your success story. I have a fellow who works with me right now. It's our third company together. I've recently told him he needs to find someone he can mentor so he can build a team of people whom he can bring along as he moves up.*

Mary Duseau
*CEO and President*
*Roka Bioscience, Inc.*

## CHAPTER EIGHT

# How to Work with a Coach or a Mentor

## When and How to Work with a Coach or Mentor

Coaching and mentoring have come a long way since the days when companies used these outside resources to help fix toxic behavior at the top of the organization. Today, coaches and mentors are widely used across all levels of the organization to help people accelerate their development and improve their performance as leaders. They do this in much the same way that athletic coaches work with players: By helping you make the most of your natural abilities and find ways to work around your weaknesses.

Imagine for a moment learning to play a game like golf, which requires knowledge of the rules, concentration, and practice in order to achieve success. Now think about what it would be like to learn how to play this game without access to an instructor or a coach. Most of us would throw our clubs up in the air in a fit of frustration. In fact, that's exactly what many of us did back in the nineties, when we didn't have access to people who could help us improve our game at work—we left corporate America to start dot.com companies.

## The Big Debate—Mentor or Coach?

Ask ten people to explain the difference between a coach and a mentor, and you will most likely get ten different answers. However, most would agree that there *is* a difference. Before you start looking around for a coach or a mentor, you must determine what specifically you are looking to gain from this type of relationship. Once you've answered this question, you'll know which direction to move toward. Here are some general guidelines to help you decide.

Mentors
- Are usually much higher up in an organization than you
- May be in a role that you aspire to be in someday
- May work in the same organization or in another organization
- Are most often selected by the person who is looking for mentoring
- Are selected based on the guidance they can give to you at a certain stage of your career or development
- Hold a position of influence that is determined by the value you place in them
- Wait for the mentoree to ask for guidance
- Are usually not compensated
- May become a lifelong advocate or friend

Coaches
- Set a strategy for your development as a leader
- Work with you to develop milestones and hold you accountable as you work toward achieving these mutually agreed-upon objectives
- Help you see blind spots that often prevent managers from achieving success
- Push you to achieve your personal best
- Help you increase your professional relationships
- Work with you as an adviser
- Drive the relationship in a proactive way
- May be provided to you by the company (Note: If coaches are paid by the company, their first obligation is to the company if a conflict of interest arises)
- Are compensated for their services
- Work with you until it is determined that you have achieved your established objectives

Terri S. Alpert, founder and CEO of UnoAllaVolta.com and CookingEnthusiast.com, has found working with a coach to be very similar to working with a personal trainer at the gym. Alpert explains,

"When I have goals for myself and I want to modify my behavior, having someone to be accountable to helps with the ongoing motivation. Changes happen as a result of changing habits. It is so much work for something to become a habit. Why not use every resource you have available to you? Resources are like tools in a toolbox. Part of managing is using your resources wisely."

## The Benefits of Working with an Outside Person

Former DeKalb Chamber of Commerce president and CEO Leonardo McClarty was excited when his board chair first suggested that he work with a coach. This was his first leadership position in which he was running the show, and it was good to know that the organization wanted to invest in him.

"For me, it's been all about accelerating the learning curve!" McClarty says. "Coaches have a much clearer lens that they see things through because they are not in it day to day," says McClarty. "They have other experience that they bring to bear because they are working with other clients who are experiencing similar challenges. Most importantly, they tell you what you *need* to hear and perhaps not what you *want* to hear."

You may be thinking, "Well, isn't that the job of my boss?" Yes and no. The boss has other responsibilities, such as accounting, HR, customer service, and so forth. She is looking at the big picture and may not always have time to give you the kind of guidance you may require, particularly if you are just starting out in management. When you have a coach, however, the focus is on you. Your time together is free of other distractions.

When McClarty played college football, his team had a number of coaches, each dedicated to a specific skill needed to play the game. This allowed each coach to focus on what he or she did best. Together, they created a winning team. We see this same game plan play out throughout corporate America: The CEO decides the game strategy and calls the plays, while managers are often coached by outside experts who are known for their ability to pull together winning teams.

Alpert uses a similar approach in her company, where anyone who wants coaching can have it. Sometimes she offers coaches to people who are not meeting expectations. "We want to give them every chance of succeeding in order to have a long-term place here," Alpert says.

She offers a coach as a resource with one caveat, however: You have to achieve the goals that have been agreed upon. Alpert has found that most people who choose not to use a coach are not truly committed to achieving the goals. If this is the case, then it's best not to waste this resource.

# What to Look for in a Coach or a Mentor

Nowadays, it seems like just about everyone is a coach or a mentor. So why not simply use the same coach your friend has been using? That may be fine, but before doing so, make sure your needs are the same and that this coach or mentor is the right fit for you. Here are some other things to look for in a coach or a mentor:

1. **Does this person's experience make the grade?**
   I don't know about you, but I certainly don't want someone coaching me on how to successfully do my first jump out of a plane if that person hasn't already done it at least a dozen times! The same holds true when selecting a coach or a mentor in business. A life coach might be great for your cousin who has decided to reenter the workforce after a leave of absence, but this person may not be appropriate for you if you're looking to learn how to become a more effective leader. You need someone who has been in the trenches and has successfully led people.
2. **Do your styles match?**
   You need to be comfortable showing this person who you truly are, and at times hearing some difficult feedback. Some coaches are known to be direct, while others take a softer approach. Knowing which style you prefer will enable you to find someone with whom you can work successfully.
3. **Is this person willing to give you a trial period?**
   It's difficult to really know if your personalities will click until you begin working together. That's why it's important to make sure whoever works with you is agreeable to a trial period. This does not mean you are entitled to a full refund should you decide partway through the engagement that you are not compatible. This simply means you have an out clause in case you need to go your separate ways.

4. **Has this person successfully helped others in similar situations?**

   What does this person's track record look like? Find out how long your potential coach has been working with people, and in what capacity. Be careful not to get too caught up in specifics, though. An excellent coach who previously helped a new manager in a manufacturing company strengthen his relationships with senior management can certainly do the same for you, even if you work in retail.

5. **Is this person available?**

   Finding a wonderful coach or mentor won't do you much good if that person does not have the time to help you. Before you enter into a relationship, clearly define your needs and ask the person whether or not your expectations are realistic given other commitments.

You may also want to consider the person's official credentials, but don't get too hung up on this. I'm often asked if a coach without certification is worth considering. In the interest of full disclosure, I do not have a coaching certification, yet I have effectively coached people for more than twenty years. Find someone who can demonstrate the achievement of similar successes, and don't worry about the three letters that may or may not be assigned to the coach's name. When you've identified someone you like, check references. If they match what you have observed, proceed. It's that simple.

# The Best Times to Work with an Outside Person

Here are a few of the most vital times to consider working with a coach or mentor.

- You are preparing yourself for a promotion.
- You need to adjust quickly to a new circumstance.
- You have employees you find challenging to manage.
- You find yourself working for a difficult boss.
- You've been assigned to a new function, office, or even country that requires you to use skills you have barely developed.
- You have performance weakness that, left unattended, could spread and negatively impact other areas of your performance.

# Does Gender Matter?

There are certainly varying beliefs regarding whether it is best to have a coach or mentor of the same sex. In many situations you may not have a choice, since there still aren't always enough women in leadership positions to go around. That being said, there may be times when specifically obtaining a mentor or a coach of the same sex is worth pursuing.

"There are many things women have to consider that men don't have to deal with," notes Mary Stutts, author of *The Missing Mentor: Women Advising Women on Power, Progress, and Priorities*[1] and Vice President External Affairs at Comcast NBCUniversal. "Women still have the primary responsibility to handle family matters. You don't often hear men talk about work/life balance. That's where having a female mentor can really come in handy for women."

However, this doesn't mean that women shouldn't take advantage of the resources that male mentors may offer. And today's male workers, who also struggle with work/life balance, may equally benefit from having a female mentor who has unlocked the secret to having a successful career while being there for her family.

# How to Find a Mentor or a Coach

Mentors can be found in many places. Begin by looking inside your company. Many organizations have established formal mentoring programs. If that is the case, then all you need to do is ask, and you will be matched with someone in the organization who has volunteered to participate in the program.

If your company doesn't have a formal program, then you will need to look outside to find a mentor. Sometimes these relationships fall into your lap. For example, perhaps you're at a conference and you meet someone who takes an interest in what you are saying. As the conversation continues, you feel a connection. Before long, that person tells you to call the next time you find yourself in a particular situation.

Other times, you might have to search high and low for an appropriate mentor. You need to put yourself in places where you will easily encounter these people. For many, this may be a conference or associa-

---

[1] "The Missing Mentor: Women Advising Women on Power, Progress and Priorities," Mary E. Stutts, Household Pub, June 2010.

tion meeting where you've identified one of the speakers as someone you would like to get to know.

Stutts says that you have to get creative. "Go to these conferences, even if you have to pay your own way, to get access to the people who are the leaders in their field. Go up to them after they have spoken and hand them something of interest. Ask them for permission to follow up for feedback," advises Stutts. For example, provide a summary of a recent study that is related to their particular area of interest. She also suggests joining a project at your company in order to have access to leaders you might not encounter otherwise.

The internet is another great resource for finding a coach or mentor. Comb through your alumni association's online directory and search for alumni who are in positions to which you aspire. Send an e-mail asking potential mentors if they might make time to meet you for a coffee before or after work. Use your LinkedIn network to search out possible mentors as well.

Don't be surprised if it takes a while to find a mentor. People are busy, and most won't immediately volunteer to take on another project. However, they may do so after they have had some time to get to know you.

## Maximizing Your Relationship with a Mentor or Coach

Before we move on, let's take a look at some specific ways you can maximize your relationship with your mentor or coach.

### WORKING WITH MENTORS

Samir Said, former founder and CEO of Social Business Bank, has invested much of his time in developing relationships with mentors who have been of great support to him in building his business. As noted, often, these relationships develop organically. You may be introduced to someone at a conference whom you seem to click with, or you may intentionally be on the lookout for this person. Said believes that the mentoring relationship must be a two-way street. He says, "You have to provide some sort of value to the mentor. This may be a small sign of appreciation, or it may involve trying to help the mentor out as well." In his situation, he has intentionally looked for connections that would be of interest to his mentors before introducing himself to them.

Stutts believes it is of utmost importance to be prepared when you meet with a mentor, and to list the specific issues you need help with. "These are busy people," notes Stutts. "Stick to the agreed-upon time frame. Get in and out of the mentor's office. Make the best use of your access by being concise. Ask very specific questions that you want the mentor to answer. If you follow this advice, the mentor will happily meet with you again."

Life coach and strategic marketer Steffi Black advises people to consider the circumstances and evaluate the best way to honor your relationship with a mentor. "In some situations, you will be better served to set up regular times to get together. In other situations, having an open-ended relationship where you can call when you need to is best," Black advises. Make sure the mentor doesn't just become a sounding board for your problems, but acts as someone who helps you reflect on the situations that arise and makes you think about how to deal with them.

Think of mentors as people who are volunteering to give of themselves. Be respectful, take only what you need, and be prepared to give back when the opportunity presents itself.

## WORKING WITH COACHES

Most coaching situations are set up for a defined period of time. Therefore, it is especially important that you make the most of your time together. To do so, you must begin with clear objectives. These are usually established together with your coach, along with ground rules, time frames, and specific goals and measures of success.

You must follow through on what you say you will do. It makes no sense to work with a coach unless you are fully committed to making the necessary changes that will give you lifelong results. If not, you will be like those people at the gym who show up, chat a bit as they go through the motions of doing what looks like exercise, and return home only to find that little has changed.

Alpert offers the following advice on effectively working with a coach: "It is important never to think the coach is going to do the work for you. The coach exists to hold up the mirror so you can see your own actions and behaviors in order to achieve your goals. This must be something you personally want to do, not something your boss thinks you should do. You have to want to grow on a personal level."

# Knowing When It's Time to Cut the Cord

Having an outside person to rely on can be great until you become too dependent or you outgrow the relationship. At this point, it makes sense to either fly on your own or find someone else who can help take you to the next level. Here are seven signs that it may be time to let go of your relationship with a mentor or coach.

1. You are not achieving the results you are hoping to achieve.
2. You feel you are no longer growing.
3. You are assigned to a new position where this person has no expertise.
4. You are afraid to make a move without checking in with your coach or mentor.
5. You are scrambling to find things to talk about.
6. It seems to be taking longer and longer for this person to return your calls.
7. You have mastered the skills you have been working on and are now able to teach others.

——————————— KEY LEARNING POINTS ———————————

- Corporate coaches are no longer reserved for executives who are behaving badly. Today, they are widely used across organizations to help employees with high potential to strengthen their leadership skills.

- There is a difference between working with a coach and working with a mentor. Before you start looking around for a coach or a mentor, you must determine what specifically you are looking to gain from this relationship. Once you've defined this, you will know how best to proceed.

- A mentor is someone who will help you without receiving any material goods in return. It's your responsibility to call upon your mentor when you need guidance.

- A coach is paid to help you. Clear objectives, along with agreed-upon ground rules, time frames, and specific goals and measures of success are the foundation of the coaching relationship.

- When selecting a coach or mentor, make sure the fit is right, especially since you will be sharing information that is of a personal nature. Look for someone who has a proven track record of helping people achieve the same types of results you are looking to achieve.

- There are many ways to find a mentor, including tapping into your organization's formal mentoring program, making connections at conferences, social networking, and searching your college alumni network.

- It is important to nourish mentoring relationships. Keep the mentor informed regarding your successes and provide acknowledgment along the way. Be respectful, take only what you need, and be prepared to give back when an opportunity presents itself to do so.

*People often ask me how you know when it's time to leave an organization. There are signs. Some are obvious and others not so much. The number one sign is when you have a pit in your stomach on Sunday night and you just don't want to go in to the office. Come Sunday afternoon after 4:00 P.M., you say, "I don't know if I can do this anymore."*

*Another sign is when your name doesn't appear on the new organization chart. This actually happened to me. During an executive presentation, a new organization chart was put up on the screen. My name was not on the chart.*

*Other signs include you are no longer getting the interesting assignments. They are going to other people. Or when the company stops investing in you and you no longer are given opportunities to further develop yourself.*

Michael Dowd
*Former CEO*
*Grand Circle Travel*

## CHAPTER NINE

# Seven Signs Your Time Is Up

## Knowing When It's Time to Go

**W**hy is it easy to see when someone around us is about to be fired, yet we don't recognize those signs when it happens to us? Perhaps you were too busy looking in front of you to notice the waves of layoffs, one of which eventually took you out. Or maybe you were hoping to turn around a situation that had gone bad. In most circumstances, it is better to leave on your own terms, as you control the outcome. However, there are times when it is best to wait out the coming storm, so you can be the recipient of a generous departing gift as you exit. The key is to be purposeful and to remain in control of your destiny. Knowing the signs that indicate a change may be in your immediate future will enable you to create the outcome that will serve you best.

## Seven Signs Your Time Is Up

Years of experience have taught me there are almost always warning signs that indicate a shift is about to happen. Here are seven of the most common signs your time is quickly coming to an end.

### SIGN NUMBER 1: YOU ARE NO LONGER IN THE LOOP

This scene may play out in different ways, but the ending is always the same. You used to be invited to participate in closed-door meetings where highly confidential matters were discussed. Lately, you notice the blinds are closed in the conference room, yet you are noting this from the *outside* of the room.

I remember this happening to me when I experienced my first layoff. Working in human resources, I was privy to all the comings and goings of the organization. Then one day I no longer had access to this information. Meetings that I normally attended went on without me. In retrospect, I should have realized that something was going on, but instead I chose to go about my business as if nothing had changed. Two weeks later, the bottom of my world fell out when I received my pink slip.

When Tracy O'Connell, associate professor of marketing communications at the University of Wisconsin–River Falls, worked in the corporate world, she went from a prized performer (based on bosses' comments and personnel reviews, promotions, and such) to someone who was apparently on the way out. She began to realize she was no longer in the loop when meetings with the boss were canceled, phone calls or e-mails were not returned, and the boss was generally unavailable to her. "I sat outside the door, hoping for a chance to ask maybe just one question, to move ahead on one thing. It was like paparazzi stalking a celebrity," states O'Connell.

If your gut tells you something has changed and your mind tries to convince you it's all in your head, then it's worth further exploration. In my experience, when it comes to matters like this, your gut is usually right. That explains why we often hear people say, "I knew it! I felt like this was coming," as they are doing the perp walk out the door, escorted by security.

## SIGN NUMBER 2: YOUR BOSS ASKS YOU TO TRAIN A "BACKUP"

At work, we often hear, "We need someone trained in case you get hit by a bus," even though we rarely hear about people *actually* getting taken out by a bus gone wild. This is frequently code for, "You're on your way out, pal. I need to make sure someone else can do your job before I fire you." If you are in this situation, you have several choices. You can do as requested without asking any questions, or you can put together a strategy for approaching the boss and learning more about why he is making this request. In most situations, people will go with option one, as this avoids conflict, even though option two is clearly the better choice.

Here's why you should talk honestly with your boss. Suppose you approached your boss in a nonconfrontational way and shared your concerns with him. This might open up a dialogue in which you learn more about areas you can quickly turn around to prevent receiving an early checkout notice. Or you may be able to negotiate a win-win deal. I've done this and it works really well, when executed properly.

Most bosses will do anything to avoid firing people. It's unpleasant and it doesn't exactly present your boss in the best light to his peers, staff, or, in some cases, the board. So if you look at this situation from your boss's point of view, you are actually doing him a favor by presenting him with a win-win situation.

It's much more difficult to fill a job when the person in the job has not been informed that her time is up. You might suggest to your boss that over the next three months (or whatever time you anticipate you will need) you will continue to perform your job while assembling a detailed procedures manual or training guide for your replacement. Offer to stay and help train your replacement. (Never mind that he may prefer you don't.) In return, ask for permission to tender your resignation, time off to interview, and whatever other terms you can negotiate, such as the bonus that is due to be paid out next month. Now, doesn't this feel more empowering than pretending there may indeed be a surge in the number of buses wiping out mid-level managers over the next six months?

## SIGN NUMBER 3: YOUR COMPANY IS TANKING

Has the owner of the company recently placed a guard on the office thermostat to save money on heating and cooling bills? Do you now have to steal office supplies from home in order to fill the supply cupboards at work? Or even worse, is the manufacturing plant standing idle while everyone waits for a miracle? Is your company losing contracts that used to be a slam dunk? These are all signs that the glory days of the company may well be behind you.

It's unlikely that a company that has fallen on hard financial times will turn around quickly. You may be forced to take action sooner rather than later, especially if you are the primary breadwinner. That's not exactly a bad thing. Often, being the first to go can be a good strategic move. You get into the employment market before it is flooded with other candidates from your industry or specialty. However, you do not have to quit in order to explore your options. You can start putting feelers out to see if you get any nibbles. Or you can turn the heat up and do a full-blown job search while continuing to earn a paycheck.

## SIGN NUMBER 4: SELF-IMPOSED BARRIERS
## BOX IN YOUR COMPANY

Product manager Donald Lester describes a no-win situation that is all too common: "Our sales team has been asked to increase sales by more than 25 percent per year. The problem is that our production facility is maxed out, order fulfillment is running way behind, and customers are getting angry and leaving. If your salary or bonus is tied to sales under these circumstances, it is time to leave. It won't get better because upper management is unwilling to spend the money needed to expand and is instead resorting to gimmicks like putting out memos that everyone needs to work harder. Under this scenario you will never make more money for your hard work in increasing sales. Time to move on."

Not everyone who is running a company is a scholar, and a number of today's leaders have never experienced what it is like to work in a recession. Many are choosing to hold on to cash, without giving enough consideration to what this may mean over the long term. A perfect example of a company that made this mistake is the now-defunct electronics retailer Circuit City. When the economy started slowing down, Circuit City decided to get rid of its 3,400 highest-paid (and almost certainly most effective) sales associates to cut its costs. This opened up the gates for competitors such as Best Buy to hire these exceptional salespeople and gain ground. Once the death spiral started, it was impossible to stop.

If you no longer believe in the decisions being made at the top of the organization, then it's time to find a company where you feel confident the lights will still be on tomorrow.

## SIGN NUMBER 5: YOUR COMPANY IS
## MERGING OR BEING ACQUIRED

In the case of a merger or acquisition, it seems easy to do the math, yet many miscalculate how things will end. Suppose you are the manager of marketing and the acquired company also happens to have a manager of marketing. What is the likelihood the organization will need two marketing managers? If I were in Vegas, I'd say the odds are slim to none. Yet people roll the dice every day, thinking they will be the one who survives the transition. These same people are shocked when they find out they weren't holding the winning hand after all.

Jill Wade, CEO of Axiom Business Advisors, LLC, has seen enough mergers and acquisitions in her lifetime to know that it's time to look at other options the moment you realize you no longer have clear duties.

"This happens a lot in mergers and acquisitions. You become a spare part," observes Wade.

The time to begin preparing for a possible exit is when a company announcement is made regarding a merger or an acquisition. Donald Lester shares a time when he worked for an organization that was going through a corporate merger. Key people flew to his location and announced everyone's job was safe. "Within three days of the announcement, you notice several people missing and the cycle repeats. Our campus had over 3,000 employees on it before the mergers started. When I left, I was one of seventy-five people remaining and they were still telling us our jobs were safe." Use your head. Put the wheels in motion. The worst that will happen is that you've got a plan in place that's ready to go with a moment's notice.

## SIGN NUMBER 6: YOUR BOSS GETS FIRED

Anytime someone above you is fired, there will be some turbulence. Some people do fine and fly right through it, while others feel as if they are going to crash at any moment. If you've got the stomach for it, you may choose to stay and ride things out.

It's important to be aware of the outside forces that could eventually take this decision out of your hands. Here is what can happen when the boss is fired: Your department may be merged with another department, which might result in your position being eliminated. Or the company may name a new boss, who brings his own people with him. If you are too closely aligned with your boss, you may eventually be asked to leave as well. Or you may wind up staying until you realize that you don't see eye to eye with the new boss.

## SIGN NUMBER 7: THERE IS NO PLACE LEFT TO GO

At some point you may realize you have gone as far as you are going to go with your present company. Most likely this will happen sooner rather than later if you work for a very small firm or a family-owned business (unless, of course, you marry into the family!). Although transitions can be difficult for some people, most would agree in hindsight that leaving at the right time was one of the best things they could have done for their career.

# Exiting with Grace—and Perhaps a Check in Hand

If you take away only one thing from this chapter, let it be this: *Always give at least two weeks' notice.* I don't care if your new employer is pressuring you to start tomorrow or if you'd love to put the screws to your old boss on the way out. Give proper notice. It may seem like a large world when you are starting out in management, but as you age you will see how small the world really is. Sometime in the future, you will be looking for a job. Your old boss will be contacted whether you like it or not, though you may never get to this stage if the hiring manager finds out you left a previous employer high and dry. That being said, always be prepared to leave the same day you give notice. Most employers will pay you for the notice time, even if you are asked not to work out your notice period. You can always call your new employer and bump up your start date if you find you are available earlier than you expected.

Company policy may state that employees are entitled to receive X, Y, and Z when they leave the company, when in fact many people are receiving U, V, and W as well. My motto is, if you don't ask, you don't get. Following are some items you can ask for. You can ask to remain on the payroll while you are receiving severance pay. This way, you can keep your health benefits in place for that much longer. You can ask your company to pay for the class you're enrolled in, even though you will no longer be an employee on the day you finish. If the company is concerned that you may take this to a lawyer, they will gladly put together a separation package that will include much more pay than what you've initially been awarded. However, in most situations this will require you to sign a separation agreement releasing the company from liability now and in the future. Note: You should *always* speak with an attorney before signing a separation agreement.

# Manage Your References Before You Need Them

People often ask me how to manage references when they've been fired. I tell them it's extremely difficult to do so after the fact. That is why it's crucial to manage your references *before* you exit. You do this by asking your boss if she is willing to write a brief letter you can use as a reference. Highlight those areas where you have excelled and ask her to include this in the letter. Better yet, offer to draft the letter for her approval.

Many of you may be thinking that no one takes reference letters seriously. After all, why would anyone show a prospective employer a letter that says anything but great things? You are right. The real value of these letters is the mindset they impose on your soon-to-be-former boss. Is this person really going to lambaste you after he's put something in writing that says you are a great employee? Probably not. Less sophisticated hiring managers may look at the letter and accept it as a sufficient reference. Most will never call your old boss for more information.

# Why Some Managers Get Nasty When You Give Notice

Often, a boss will become hostile when you give notice. Here are some reasons why this happens.

Your boss:

- Is fearful that he will not be able to find someone to replace you quickly.
- May be afraid her inadequacies will become apparent once you are gone.
- Is overwhelmed and can't imagine adding your work to her workload.
- Fears your departure will reflect negatively on his leadership.
- Feels left behind. You are going on to something better and he is not.
- Feels betrayed. Perhaps your boss helped you get where you are today, and now you are leaving her.

As you can see, none of these reasons really has anything to do with you. Finish what needs to be done and exit as gracefully as you arrived.

## Other Things to Think about Before Leaving

People say you should never quit a job until you have another job. I would say it depends on the situation. If you've got the type of job that is so demanding you cannot possibly conduct a job search while employed, then you may need to exit before you have something lined up. Or if the environment is so toxic that it is affecting your health, then choose life.

Some reasons you may want to stay until you find another job include the following:

- A potential employer is more likely to offer you more money in order to get you to leave your current employer.
- A potential employer is likely to match the vacation time you are now entitled to.
- You are more marketable. Everyone seems to want what others have, particularly when it comes to serenading an employee away from the competition.
- You will not have to pay 100 percent of the cost for health insurance.
- You may be approaching a vesting period that will entitle you to receive additional money in your retirement plan.
- You may wind up staying long enough to receive another bonus or a raise in salary.
- A bad boss might leave, and you may then decide to stay.

## Should You Resign Before You Get Fired?

There may be times when an employer is concerned how others will react to someone in the organization being fired. Often, a manager will offer an employee the option to tender his letter of resignation rather than be terminated. Is this in your best interest? It depends on how you negotiate your exit. In many states, if you resign, you are not eligible to collect unemployment benefits. Can you afford to give this up? Here is something else a lot of people do not know. You can accept the offer to resign with the contingency that your company will not fight your unemployment claim. If they agree, get this in writing.

It's never easy to leave an organization, especially if your departure isn't on your own terms or timeline. Use each experience to better yourself. I wouldn't be in the position I'm in today—successfully helping organizations improve their people, productivity, and profitability—without having experienced being suddenly in charge. Remember, each encounter shapes who you become, as both a person and a leader.

—————————— KEY LEARNING POINTS ——————————

- There are usually signs along the way indicating that your time may be up. Signs include: You are no longer in the loop; you are asked to train a "backup"; the company is sinking quickly; poor decisions are being made at the top; a merger or acquisition is pending; your boss is fired; or there is no place left for you to go.

- You can exit the company with more than your vacation pay in hand. Consider what you feel entitled to and ask away, keeping in mind that if you don't ask, you certainly won't receive.

- The time to manage your references is before you need them. Always ask for a letter of recommendation, even if the separation isn't completely voluntary. Make it easy for your boss to say yes. Offer to draft the letter for his approval.

- Understanding why some managers get nasty when people give notice will enable you to remain composed as you work your way out the door. Often, this behavior is related to fear or occurs because your boss is feeling overwhelmed.

- Ideally, it is best to have another job lined up before you tender your resignation. In reality, this is not always possible. Weigh the pros and cons of leaving sooner rather than later before you make your final decision.

- Before agreeing to a forced resignation, understand the ramifications. There may be times where one option is clearly better than another.

- *Always* have an attorney review a separation agreement before signing.

- Every encounter shapes who you are and who you become. Use every experience to redefine your future.

*Now that you've mastered **Managing UP**, flip the book over and begin working on the skills you will need to successfully **Manage DOWN**.*

Now that you've reviewed and practiced what you must do in order to effectively **Manage DOWN**, flip the book over and review what you must do to continue to successfully **Manage UP**.

# Praise for *Suddenly in Charge, Second Edition*

"The best advice is simple, direct, and immediately actionable. Roberta delivers on all this and more. A lifesaving guide for any new manager"!

—**Marshall Goldsmith—The international best-selling author or editor of 35 books including *What Got You Here Won't Get You There* and *Triggers*.**

"Matuson offers practical, no-nonsense advice for some of the most common situations leaders find ourselves managing through at some point in our careers, it's like having a coach on your bookshelf! Grab a copy for yourself, and one for a friend—they'll thank you!"

—**Sandy Rezendes, Chief Learning Officer, Citizens Financial Group, Inc.**

"Sad to say, doing your job well isn't sufficient for success. Unless you also learn to navigate critical relationships with your boss and your employees, everything else is in jeopardy. Consider *Suddenly in Charge* your lifeline, helping you make sense of the complex terrain of the modern workplace."

—**Dorie Clark, author of *Reinventing You* and *Stand Out*, and adjunct professor at Duke University's Fuqua School of Business**

"Wow! I didn't think it was possible, but the second edition of *Suddenly in Charge* is even better than the first! Roberta's no-nonsense approach is exactly what is needed in the fast-paced world of work. A must read for every manager."

—**Jay Hargis, Former Director of Learning and Development at Tufts Medical Center, and adjunct professor at NYU.**

"Roberta understands that people are the heart of any business. As a Boston based family business owner, I completely agree with her. I would highly recommend this book to leaders and anyone who heads up a business."

—**Peter Rinnig, owner QRST's**

"In *Suddenly in Charge*, Roberta does a fabulous job of weaving practical action steps with extraordinarily insightful knowledge that we all need. Having led people and organizations for over 25 years in the US Navy and various industries, I can without a doubt recommend *Suddenly in Charge* to anyone wanting to improve their leadership and followership capacity. And, as a father of three soon to enter the workforce, this will be a must read at the Koonce household! Thanks, Roberta, for sharing your wisdom!"

—**Bob Koonce, Co-Author of *Extreme Operational Excellence: Applying the US Nuclear Submarine Culture to Your Organization*, Former Nuclear Submarine Commander and Principal Officer, High Reliability Group LLC**

"I have personally worked with Roberta, she assisted me in evaluating and changing my team. I now have the high performing team I wanted. This book can do the same for you!"

**—Ronald Bryant, President Baystate Noble Hospital**

"*Suddenly in Charge* is a must read for both experienced and new leaders. You'll learn practical tips on how to navigate up, down and across your network and most importantly the value of strong relationships with yourself, your team, and the business."

**—Sandy Allred, Kimberly-Clark, Senior Director, Talent Management**

# Suddenly
# in Charge

Managing Up,
## MANAGING DOWN,
### Succeeding All Around

*Revised and Updated*

ROBERTA CHINSKY MATUSON

NICHOLAS BREALEY
PUBLISHING

BOSTON • LONDON

First published in 2017 by Nicholas Brealey Publishing
An imprint of John Murray Press

An Hachette company

23 22 21 20 19 18 17    1 2 3 4 5 6 7 8 9 10

**Library of Congress Control Number: 2017012373**

ISBN 978-1-473-65605-5
U.S. eBook ISBN 978-1-857-88467-8
U.K. eBook ISBN 978-1-473-64412-0

Printed in the United States of America

Nicholas Brealey Publishing policy is to use papers that are natural, renewable
and recyclable products and made from wood grown in sustainable forests. The
logging and manufacturing processes are expected to conform to the environ-
mental regulations of the country of origin.

Nicholas Brealey Publishing          Nicholas Brealey Publishing
Carmelite House                           Hachette Book Group
50 Victoria Embankment                        53 State Street
London EC4Y 0DZ                    Boston, MA 02109, USA
Tel: 020 3122 6000                      Tel: (617) 263 1834

www.nicholasbrealey.com

# How to Navigate
# This Book

*Once you've reviewed and practiced what you must do in order to effectively* **Manage DOWN,** **FLIP THE BOOK OVER** *and review what you must do to continue to successfully* **Manage UP.**

Why is it that so many people believe everyone should have to go through the same school of hard knocks that they've suffered through? This is common in the field of medicine, where young interns are subject to the same stresses their mentors have gone through just because it's viewed as the rite of passage. We also see this in management, where people of all ages are dropped into their chairs and expected to know exactly what to do by osmosis. I'm here to tell you that the rite of passage is wrong, and I'm doing something about it.

I've devoted an entire section to *Managing DOWN* because I believe most people who take on the responsibilities of management *really* want to do a good job and are capable of doing so, with proper guidance. The problem is that in this fast-paced world no one has time to show you the ropes. Therefore, you must take control and learn how to become an effective manager on your own in order to thrive in the business world.

Management is not for the faint of heart, nor is it for people who believe if you want something done right, you have to do it yourself. It's ideally suited for those who are committed to helping others succeed. It requires patience, diligence, and, most certainly, as you'll see, a good sense of humor.

There will be days when you'll feel like you are riding the crest of a wave and other days when you might feel as if the next wave is going to take you out. Don't despair. Thumb through this section of the book and remind yourself that through practice and determination, you can do this.

Now hang on. It's going to be one heck of a ride!

# Contents

## CHAPTER THREE

# Purpose: The Secret Ingredient that Will Separate You from the Pack

## CHAPTER FOUR

# Talent Magnetism

## CHAPTER FIVE

# Guard Your Exits: How to Prevent Your Employees from Taking the Next Flight Out

**CHAPTER SIX**

# Generation Integration

## Leveraging Workplace Differences into Opportunities    69

**CHAPTER SEVEN**

# Dealing with Difficult Employees

## Strategies to Keep You Sane during Insane Times    81

# Introduction to Managing Down

**M**anagement looks really easy, doesn't it? You're awarded a title, and, if you are lucky, an office, and away you go. You bark some orders here and there and then you sit back until it's time to give another directive. Of course everyone does *exactly* what you ask of them, because you are the person in charge. If this were really the case, everyone would want to be a manager!

Being an effective manager is a lot more complicated than the scenario I described above. That's because the only behavior you can control is your own. In the following chapters, we'll discuss exactly what it is going to take for you to succeed as a first-time manager or to become a business owner who inspires his people to do their best. There is no one-size-fits-all model of management. You will need to try on different styles until you find the one that is the perfect fit for you and the environment you are working in. Throughout your career you will find yourself making adjustments as you grow as a leader.

My leadership skills have marinated over time. I know exactly when I need to turn up the heat and when it's best to let things simmer. Along the way, I have had my share of disasters. But I viewed each and every situation as an opportunity to fine-tune my craft. My hope is that you will do the same. Leadership is a skill set that can be learned, but only if you are willing to practice and learn from your mistakes. Take the pieces of advice that follow in this book and use the ingredients that feel right to you. Experiment and create your own recipe for success!

---

See the Foreword in the Managing Up side of this book, page xi, to read what bestselling author Alan Weiss has to say about *Suddenly in Charge* and Roberta Matuson's approach to preparing you for success.

---

I will never forget the day that I was tossed into management. I walked into the office as just another employee and left that day as a member of senior management. Here's my story.

I had a very close relationship with my boss, with whom I had worked at another company. She had come to my rescue and offered me a job as a human resources generalist when I had suddenly found myself unemployed in the midst of a recession. We worked side by side to build a state-of-the-art human resources department for a commercial real estate firm that eventually went public.

My boss appeared to be doing well in her job and had the full support of the executive management team. At least I thought she did. There were absolutely no indications that one day my boss would be there and the next day she would be gone. But that is exactly what happened one day in 1983.

On a sunny spring morning, I received a call from the vice president's secretary requesting my presence in his office. This seemed a bit unusual, as I had never been called to his office without my supervisor. I assumed she would be there, waiting for my arrival. I was caught completely off guard when the VP closed his door and began speaking with me, before my supervisor arrived. Without any fanfare, he informed me that my boss was no longer with the company, as of the evening before. That was the entire conversation. No explanation and no directions. I paused for a moment to think. And then I did what I thought any other twenty-

*four-year-old would do: I asked for her job. Imagine my surprise when he granted my request and gave me the title of acting director of human resources! Six months later, I was promoted to director.*

*I still remember how I felt that day when I found out that I was suddenly in charge of an entire department, including five peers who were now my direct reports. I felt like I was at the top of a roller coaster waiting to descend. I was scared, yet excited about the plunge I was about to take. These are probably similar to the feelings you are experiencing if you have been tossed into management.*

*I began my first ninety days by focusing on improving my technical skills so that I could be competent in my job. This is a mistake many new managers commonly make. In hindsight, I should have spent that time developing strong relationships with others in the organization, especially those on my team.*

*I've learned a lot about management and leadership over the past twenty-five years. Some of my knowledge was acquired through further formal education, but most I learned on the job, through trial and error. Your journey will be different from mine, and you'll make your own mistakes along the way. But at least you'll have something that I never had: A roadmap to guide you safely through the twists and turns you will experience in this new terrain called management.*

Roberta Chinsky Matuson
*President*
*Matuson Consulting*

# Welcome to Management

## Now What the Heck Do I Do?

ongratulations! You've just been tagged and now you're it! You are now a boss. Welcome to the game of management. To win in this game, you must quickly figure out the rules on your own, because there is no playbook that will provide you with all the moves you need to come out a winner. Maybe it's a good thing there is no playbook, because just when you think you've got the game figured out, it changes! For example, most economists and businesspeople did not predict the deep recession of 2009. In the years prior to the recession, most of the world was experiencing a period of strong economic growth. Leaders became quite comfortable managing at a time when they could pretty much buy their way in and out of any situation.

Here are some examples of the ways managers have used money to deal with management issues, a strategy that didn't require much in the way of leadership skills. Suppose a key employee said she was leaving for another organization; a manager could make a competitive counteroffer and usually keep this person. When money wasn't an issue in business, managers could follow Google's corporate model of attracting candidates by offering perks such as an on-site doctor and dentist; complimentary massages and yoga; free lunch from a five-star caterer; and bringing in a sushi chef. Then the game changed. Companies all around the world were forced to tighten their belts and get rid of the fat in their organizations, including the weekly donut run. Managers could no longer motivate employees by promising extravagant perks, and they were scrambling to figure out quickly how to do more with less. A new game was in play, and the old rules no longer mattered.

Oh, what a difference a few years make. In many parts of the world, the economy is humming. Here in the U.S., many cities are experiencing record-low unemployment rates. Companies are once again pulling out all the stops as they look to buy talent. But here's the thing—there will always be companies with better perks than yours or with higher salary ranges. But don't despair. There appears to be a vast shortage of great leaders. In a recent TinyPulse New Year Employee Report, 1,000 working Americans shared their workplace wishes for the New Year.[1] Participants were asked what one thing they wished they could change about their manager. The second most popular answer was to have their manager quit. This response aligns with what I see in my consulting practice. Many enthusiastic employees are working for managers who are unclear about how to connect with their people in a way that is memorable for the right reasons.

You have an opportunity to become the type of manager who can thrive in *any* economy. Managers who were let go in the downturn are wishing they had spent a little less time watching the football game from the company's skybox and more time on the playing field, leading their team to victory. Let's look at some basics that will help you to build a strong foundation as a manager. I'll also share ways you can connect with the hearts and minds of your employees and create a magnetic relationship that will have your people sticking to you for years to come.

## Tossed into Management

How many careers can you think of where people are thrown into a job with little preparation and expected to perform as if they've been in that role forever? This certainly doesn't occur in the medical field, where practitioners are required to spend years learning about the human body and everything that can possibly go wrong. Nurses, physicians, and medical technicians all must complete practicums and pass state board exams before they can treat patients on their own. These professionals must also take a certain number of continuing education courses each year to keep their licenses current. Skilled laborers, like plumbers and electricians, are required to work as apprentices before they are granted licenses to practice their trade. In many states,

---

[1] TinyPulse. "New Year Employee Report, 2015." https://www.tinypulse.com/landing-page/2015-new-year-employee-report.

they too are required to take refresher courses in their field in order to keep their credentials current. Yet when it comes to being a manager, there is no standard education or training that is required before you take the reins.

You may not be in a situation where you are dealing with life and death on a daily basis. However, one wrong move and the game could be over before you've even gotten started. The last thing you want to hear your boss say is, "Time of death, 14:00," as he escorts you out of the building along with your belongings.

If you are reading this book, you are off to a good start, as you have already recognized the importance of taking control of your own destiny. When the great recession hit, management training programs went the way of 401(K) matches. Companies have reinstated 401(K) matches but not management training programs. My sense is formal management programs will remain a thing of the past. Bosses are too busy doing their jobs (and the jobs of those who are fleeing the organization to work elsewhere) to provide helpful advice. To thrive, or even survive, you must take matters into your own hands. Let's begin by looking at what you need to do in your first ninety days on the job to lay a firm foundation for long-term success.

## The First Ninety Days

Let's get one thing straight. The assumption that the first ninety days are the honeymoon period is a fallacy, and here's why: The decision to award the position to you may not have been unanimous. Or, there may be people in the organization who believe the job should have been theirs. In either case, it is important to keep in mind that some in the organization may not be interested in helping you to succeed. However, in most cases you can overcome this by quickly establishing yourself as a leader and showing management that their decision to promote you was the right one. We'll discuss how to do this in more detail throughout this chapter.

Keep in mind that the first ninety days will set the stage for your performance as a manager. This is when a company will be looking for you to shine and deliver results. If you fail to build momentum from the get-go, you will face an uphill climb for the rest of your tenure. Effective, experienced managers know this is the time to work hard to build productive working relationships in the organization, establish credibility, and secure some early wins.

# How to Build Productive Relationships

Ask any effective manager how she was able to succeed, and you will hear her talk about the people she works with. That is because you cannot be an effective manager without having earned the support of others. Otherwise you will find yourself in the situation of leading without anyone actually following you or, worse, trying to operate without the support of your own manager. That is why it is important to begin building productive relationships the minute you are inducted into the ranks of management.

Here are seven ways to quickly establish productive working relationships:

## 1. TRUST ME—RELATIONSHIPS ARE BUILT ON TRUST

Have you ever worked with someone you didn't trust? Perhaps this person said one thing, but his actions or behaviors indicated something else. You may find that you often question this person's motives or intentions.

As an employee or coworker, how willing were you to do what this person asked of you? If you are like most people, you probably were not burning the midnight oil to fulfill his requests.

Relationships are based on trust. Without trust, there can be no commitment. Leaders who have established high levels of trust find that their employees are willing to do whatever it takes to get the job done. That's why it is imperative that you invest the necessary time in establishing trusting relationships, especially during your first ninety days on the job.

## 2. FIRST IMPRESSIONS COUNT

It is only natural to be excited when you've just been promoted. You may want to shout from the rooftops or, worse yet, plaster the details of your significant achievement on your Facebook page. Resist the temptation to boast, as coworkers who are now subordinates may be among your social media connections. The last thing you want to do is rub salt in the wound of a jilted coworker, whose support you will need to succeed in your new role.

This is certainly a time when all eyes are upon you. It's only natural to feel a bit anxious, but any nervousness will dissipate as you gain a few wins under your belt. Be confident. You've been selected for this

job because others believe you have the ability to figure it out! Now go out and make a good first impression. A surefire way to make a positive first impression is to ask questions and involve your employees in creating a high-functioning team. Become known as someone who truly listens to the opinions and perspectives of others.

## LIFE IN THE TRENCHES

Lisa Broesch, president of Actualize Consulting Group in Orlando, Florida, recalls her first foray into management:

> When I was twenty-two years old, I was promoted to a position as 'acting supervisor' for a Fortune 50 company. I had never previously held a leadership position, and skipped the "lead and assistant supervisor" positions altogether.
>
> Initially, I was given almost no direction or training, other than being told to "kick butt and take names." It was certainly a challenge as I went through years of trial and error leadership "styles" and frustration, before I finally figured out a consistent method that was extremely effective and suited my personality and values. What a treat it would've been to have an effective guide in place from the outset of my career!

## 3. JUMP INTO THE TRENCHES

You may have heard a rumor that once you are in management, you no longer need to work in the trenches. That may be true. However, you'll quickly gain the respect of your team if you show them you are willing to work side by side with them in order to achieve departmental goals. This approach is also a great way to get to know the strengths and weaknesses of your employees, as you will be able to see their work firsthand rather than relying on comments in their personnel files.

While it may be tempting to hide out in your new office, plotting your next move up the organizational ladder or demanding a 10 percent increase in sales now that you are in charge, your time will be better spent being visible and gaining the input of your team members. You want to get a read from those producing the work before making commitments that may not be achievable.

Step away from your keyboard and you will be amazed by what you will learn. Even the smartest computer in the world can't give you a clear picture of what your employees are really thinking and what

they are capable of doing. Engaging with them will help you to build solid relationships.

## 4. BE RESPECTFUL

It may sound obvious, but in this fast-paced world so many managers bark orders, rather than asking their employees to do things in a respectful manner. Confident leaders do not need to yell at their employees in order to get them to take action. Nor do they need to chew them out in front of others so the rest of the team hears the message loud and clear.

Think about someone in your organization you look up to, and jot down a few words that would describe his management style. I'm guessing the word "respectful" is on this list. Now think about someone in your organization who manages by fear. Which person seems to get more done? Which manager do you think has employees volunteering to stay late or come in on weekends to complete projects? More than likely, it is the manager who has the respect of his workers. He probably achieves dramatically greater results than the manager who has failed to earn the respect of his people.

## 5. FLEX YOUR STYLE OF MANAGEMENT

You may think that since you are now in charge, your staff will need to adjust their work styles to yours. However, the opposite is actually true. Effective managers have learned (sometimes the hard way) that they must adjust their style of management in order to build productive relationships. Here's an example of what I mean by this. You may prefer to brainstorm by sending e-mails back and forth until all the alternatives have been laid out. However, you may have some employees who come up with their best ideas when they are able to draw from the energy of others in a meeting or through webcasting. If you keep sending e-mails to these people, you may find that in the end, the only person hitting the reply button is you. If you continue to force people to adjust to your style, eyeballs will roll, frustration levels will escalate, and valuable time will be wasted.

Another alternative is to find a healthy balance between the various styles on your team. You might ask team members to e-mail you their top five suggestions and then compile a list that can be used to stimulate conversation at a meeting you have scheduled to discuss the project. This approach lets your people know that you are willing to meet them halfway, which is something we must often do to maintain healthy relationships.

## 6. LISTEN MORE, TALK LESS

Have you ever noticed how some bosses do lots of talking and very little listening? No wonder employee productivity is down! Imagine how many fewer meetings we would all have to attend if we did more listening and a lot less talking. If you try speaking less and listening more, you will immediately gain the respect of your staff and others in the organization.

For some people, this shift may be a bit challenging. The next time you are in a meeting, place a check mark on a piece of paper every time you are tempted to interrupt someone or, even worse, answer your cell phone while others are sharing their ideas. Warning: This exercise may require more than one piece of paper!

People enjoy talking to good listeners. This skill will serve you well as you move up in the organization and interact with high-level customers as well as members of the executive team.

## 7. HELP OTHERS SHINE

One of the biggest differences between being a worker and a manager is the way your performance will be measured. Employees are measured by the work they do. A good portion of a manager's performance rating will be based on *how well she inspires others to perform*.

As a manager, your focus should be on making sure the light is shining on the individuals who are contributing most to your team. You can do this by letting your customers or others in the organization know that one of your employees has come up with a great idea that will improve your customers' condition, rather than letting people assume the idea came from you. You'll gain even more points if you do this with the employee by your side. Remember to thank, reward, and recognize the contributions of those who help you succeed so that they remain inspired to give you their all.

# Establishing Credibility

Some managers mistakenly believe that credibility automatically comes with the title of manager. These same people are no longer in management! Credibility, as defined by the Merriam-Webster dictionary, is "the quality or power of inspiring belief." People may believe that you are technically or operationally sound, but now you must demonstrate that you have what it takes to be an effective leader. Credibility is something that must be earned continuously.

This lesson is often learned the hard way, particularly by those who have been promoted based on their technical knowledge or sales ability. People in these situations may continue to operate as if they were still in a line job. They remain technical experts or they breathe their own exhaust as they race around the organization with their sales awards in hand.

It goes without saying that you need to have a good understanding of the operation you will be managing. However, that is yesterday's news. Moving forward, you must concentrate your efforts on establishing yourself as a credible leader.

## Creating Credibility

You have to believe that you are capable of mastering the art of management. Otherwise, why would anyone else believe in you? Toss off that little guy on your shoulder who keeps whispering negative words into your ear, and prepare for success! Here are some ways to quickly establish credibility.

1. **Be yourself**—By that, I mean be authentic. Don't try to emulate the exact style and personality of the person whose job you are filling, or others will question your authenticity. Instead, build on the strengths that have helped you achieve this milestone and make a name for yourself based on the skills and values *you* bring to the position.

   Resist the temptation to become the exact replica of your boss, no matter how well respected he is in the organization. Emulating your boss may backfire, as you will be seen as an extension of your boss rather than as a leader yourself. However, there is nothing wrong with taking best practices you have learned from your supervisor and adjusting them to your own style of leadership.

2. **Be truthful**—The quickest way to lose credibility is to be caught in a lie. So why risk losing everything you've worked so hard to build by making one avoidable mistake? No one expects you to be perfect, but they do expect you to be truthful. If you are asked a question for which you do not have the answer, simply say so. Let the person who is asking the question know that you will need time to research the answer, and set up a time to get back to her. If you still don't have a response by the time you've agreed to follow up, then let the person know you are still researching the question and will get back to her shortly. Keep your commitment

to follow up. This will help you earn the reputation of being a leader who is responsive to her people.

3. **Take time to work side by side with your staff**—Working alongside your employees will allow you to experience what it is like to be in their shoes. You'll see firsthand the daily challenges they face in their jobs. Resist the temptation to offer advice on how they can do their jobs better. Instead, seek input on what it is they need in order to be more successful.

    Former restaurant manager Derrick Hayes was lucky enough to be tossed into management with a fast-food company that believed managers needed to learn every aspect of the operation in order to manage their stores effectively. Hayes started his restaurant management career working the grill. The experience proved humbling. "My people knew that I knew what was going on in the restaurant because I had the experience of working side by side with them," states Hayes. This made it easier for Hayes to gain their respect. His people knew there wasn't a job in the restaurant that he hadn't done or couldn't do. This is how you build credibility with your team.

4. **Match your actions with your words**—This is a bigger problem than most people realize. According to a 1967 study conducted by UCLA Professor Albert Mehrabian, up to 93 percent of communication effectiveness is determined by nonverbal clues. Nonverbal communications range from facial expressions to body language. Some experts argue that this percentage is more in the range of 70 percent. However, all seem to agree that body language plays a greater role in communication than spoken words. Give great care to your body language and tone when communicating with others to ensure that the message you intend to send is the message that others are receiving. For example, suppose you ask an employee what he thinks can be done to solve a quality issue that is delaying the release of a new product. Halfway through the conversation, you turn your back to look for your missing phone. What message do you think the employee is receiving? How likely is this employee to continue to research and present viable solutions to this critical problem, given the behaviors he has just observed?

Today's managers have even more distractions than those whose footsteps they are following. Computers and smartphones have proven a double-edged sword in the workplace. While these devices have certainly increased productivity, they have also significantly altered people's expectations regarding deadlines and response times.

I entered management at a time when computers were beginning to appear on the desks of managers and e-mail was just beginning to catch on. Home computers were rare, and if an e-mail was sent out late Friday afternoon, no one expected a response until Monday morning. Today, managers are receiving e-mails and text messages 24/7. The expectation of an instant response upon receipt has had a significant impact on the quality of conversations in the workplace. How many times has someone stopped to respond to an incoming cell phone call or text message while in conversation with you? How often have you turned away during a face-to-face conversation to see whose name is appearing on your caller ID? These behaviors, whether consciously being done or not, are sending mixed messages to those you are in conversation with. They are diluting the message you may be trying to send.

Your attempts to build a team where everyone feels valued may be falling short based on the behaviors you are displaying on a daily basis. Think about this the next time a "ding" sounds from your computer or smartphone, and adjust your actions. You've got all day, or even into the night, to answer that e-mail, whereas you have only a limited amount of time to speak to the person in front of you.

## Productive Relationships Self-Assessment

The intent of this self-assessment is to help you learn more about your own leadership skills. Knowing your strengths and weaknesses can help you identify the areas to focus on in order to build productive relationships with your staff, as well as with peers and those above you in the organization.

Rate your answers with the numeric value for each statement given below.

| Evaluation | Agree | Somewhat Agree | Disagree |
|---|---|---|---|
| | 3 | 2 | 1 |
| 1. In conversations I tend to do most of the talking. | | | |
| 2. I can still succeed without the support of others. | | | |

| Evaluation | Agree | Somewhat Agree | Disagree |
|---|---|---|---|
| | 3 | 2 | 1 |
| 3. My technical/operations knowledge gives me *all* the credibility I need to be successful in management. | | | |
| 4. I share my opinions first and then ask others for input. | | | |
| 5. I am the smartest person on my team. | | | |
| 6. I'd be hard pressed to perform the work of my subordinates. | | | |
| 7. My method of communication is based on my preference rather than the preferred style of the person I am communicating with. | | | |
| 8. I hesitate to ask for advice from subordinates. | | | |
| 9. I multitask when others are speaking with me. | | | |
| 10. I am known as a leader who is to be feared. | | | |

### Scoring:

Add your scores up to see how you fare.

- If your total score is between 10 and 15, then you are off to a great start!
- If you scored between 16 and 20, you're doing okay. You may want to keep an eye on things or step up your game.
- A score of 21 to 30 indicates you need to take immediate action!

**Note:** An individual score of 3 in any of these areas is worth a closer look. For example, if you agreed with the statement, "I am known as a leader who is to be feared," then it is worth examining what about your management style causes others to feel this way about you. Being known as someone others fear will directly affect your ability to attract, motivate, and retain top players for your team.

- You can do this! Many others have been tossed into management and have not only survived, but have thrived.

- There is no such thing as a ninety-day honeymoon period for new managers. This is the time when you must demonstrate that management's decision to promote you was the right choice.

- Focus your efforts during your first ninety days on building solid working relationships.

- What got you here won't keep you here. You've already established that you are technically competent or have strong operational knowledge. People are now waiting to see how credible a leader you will be.

- Your credibility is based on your words and behavior. These two areas of communication must be congruent, or your credibility will suffer.

- Credibility is not something you earn overnight, although it is something you can destroy in one day. Be mindful of how your words and actions have a direct impact on how others perceive you, on a daily basis.

There are three key lessons to keep in mind as you move from employee to team leader. They are:

1. You never fail until you quit trying.
2. Do something. Lead, follow, or get out of the way.
3. No one cares how much you know until they know how much you care.

The hardest position I ever had was when I became a supervisor to people who were my peers. I thought people would respect me and come to me with questions because I was now their boss. Instead, they took their questions to leaders other than me. I was more focused on showing them I was the right guy for the job, when I should have been working on earning their trust.

When people go from employee to a leader they seem to forget what things were like before they were promoted into management. Admittedly, I was one of these people. I started to ask people to do things I never did and I knew were not realistic. For example, asking people to make quotas that were impossible to make. Then reprimanding them when they didn't make quota.

I now understand the errors of my way and make it a point to set realistic terms. If I ask someone to do something that is a huge stretch, I'll be with them 100 percent of the way. I take the approach that we are going to work on this together.

Randy Johnson
SVP of Sales and Marketing
Edenred Commuter Benefits Solutions

# From Me to We

## It's *Really* Not about You!

E ven star quarterbacks, like the New England Patriots' Tom Brady, know that you cannot score consistently without a strong team behind you. The same holds true in management. So why do so many newly promoted managers fail to transition from a mindset of "It's all about me" to one that acknowledges that "It's all about us"?

I've witnessed a number of situations where newly minted managers started heading down the field without looking back to see if anyone was following them. The result was always disaster. In some cases, the manager was able to recover from this fumble. For every one who recovered, however, there were two more on the sidelines who never got a chance to play again. At least not for the same team.

## Why Engage Your Employees?

Extensive research has been conducted by Gallup and others that shows engaged employees are more productive and profitable, provide high levels of customer service, and are less likely to leave the company when tempted by generous offers from other firms. For our purposes, engaged employees are those who have an emotional attachment and commitment to their work. They are motivated to give their all to the task at hand, without the need for constant prodding.

As a new leader, you have the opportunity to create a work environment where your employees are highly engaged. By doing so, you will create a productive team where employee turnover is something that happens to some other manager.

I know some of you may be thinking that there is no way you will be able to turn around the disengaged team you've just inherited. If this is your mindset, then you are probably right. But for those of you who believe you can do whatever you set your mind to, here is proof that it can be done.

Barry Maher, founder of Helendale, California–based Barry Maher & Associates, once took a position as a sales manager with a Fortune 100 company, having been told his new unit had been first in the division the year before. Upon his arrival, he discovered that the top salesperson in the region had recently transferred out and that the six-person unit had three floundering rookies. The year he took over, the unit was dead last in the region. "Morale would have had to improve greatly to reach abominable," notes Maher. "In my first meeting with my new unit, I told them that within one year they were going to be the number one unit in the region. Within less than a year, they were there," states Maher. When asked how he built morale and employee engagement, Maher responded by saying that he didn't. His employees did: "I just made it possible for them to do so." Maher did this by:

1. **Demonstrating faith in his people.** Maher made it clear to his team that he truly believed that individually and collectively they had the capability to be the best. Then he acted as if that were true.
2. **Showing his loyalty to his team.** He fought for them and championed them in the division and in the company. He had their best interests at heart.
3. **Working for his employees.** Maher acted on the belief that he was there to make them successful and supported them in every way he could.
4. **Praising and rewarding his people for their accomplishments.** He made sure the company did the same.
5. **Creating a team mentality.** Maher set up a mentoring program that went beyond the constant training he was doing. He made sure that no one who wanted or needed help was ever left alone with a problem.
6. **Making it okay to fail.** In the process, he realized he could never help his team overcome their fear of failure *unless* he could first overcome his own fear of failure: "If I was afraid of failure, they would also be afraid."
7. **Making work fun.** He made having fun on the job and in the accounts a priority. "We had all kinds of contests. Some serious,

some silly," notes Maher. "A salesperson who enjoys what he is doing will sell more."

## Three Types of Employees

| Highly Engaged | Employees feel highly committed to the organization. They are willing to go above and beyond the call of duty to move the organization forward. |
|---|---|
| Moderately Engaged | Employees do what they are asked and not much more. If pushed hard enough, they will propel forward, but will relapse the moment the pressure is off. |
| Disengaged | Employees have "checked out" and they are making sure those around them follow suit. They are undermining the progress made by those who are still engaged. |

## HOW DO YOUR EMPLOYEES FARE?

Are your employees engaged? Use this list of questions as a guideline for assessing the level of engagement for each of your employees.

- Does the employee consistently perform at a high level?
- Does the employee demonstrate she is clear about the desired outcomes of her role and how it fits into the rest of the organization?
- Is the employee willing to challenge the status quo to achieve outstanding results?
- Does the employee's demeanor show a high level of enthusiasm and energy?
- Is the employee always looking for ways to add value to the assignment he has been given?
- Does the employee's behavior consistently indicate he is committed to the goals of the organization, team members, and role?
- Does the employee feel she has the ability to make a difference?

# Reality Check

It's been a rocky road in management over the past decade. Managers have been forced to put on their hard hats and dig out of some pretty big holes created by their leaders' bad decisions or by economic realities. Every one of my clients experienced downsizing due to the economic downturn, wage freezes and pay cuts, high levels of employee stress, or some combination of these. Most recently, my clients have had to deal with the challenges associated with attracting and retaining top talent at a time where talent is next to impossible to find. Leaders are under enormous pressure to deliver results with or without proper staff levels. (We'll cover the attraction and retention of talent in more detail in chapters 4 and 5.) Yet every day, they go to the office and continue to work toward achieving their mission and strategic goals, providing exceptional customer service and keeping productivity levels high enough to survive these challenging times. Some have done better than others. Here's an example of a company that has stayed the course and has not let the economy affect the respectful way they treat their people.

One client of mine, family-owned company Winston Flowers, knows a lot about forming relationships that last a lifetime. This company, which was started in 1944, has gone from a pushcart business on Newbury Street to a Boston institution. The firm considers each new connection to be a potential long-term relationship. Employees are treated like family at Winston Flowers. "More than a few of our employees have grown up with Winston's, having been part of our family for more than twenty years. We are always on the lookout for talent and find it in people from a wide variety of backgrounds. We take pleasure and pride in watching many of these creative individuals develop into leaders of the floral industry," states co-owner Ted Winston.

Winston offers the following sage advice to newly minted managers to help them cultivate lifelong relationships with their employees:

- **Make every single moment count**—Always do as much as you can to effect positive change.
- **Lead by example**—Behave as you would want your employees to behave, but also understand that your role is different from that of your employees.

- **Make sure you have the right people**—Hire for fit, train for skill. When you find the right people, it is important to welcome them and provide useful orientation, so they immediately feel connected to your culture.
- **Get to know your people's strengths**—Build on strengths, rather than weaknesses. Your return will be that much greater.
- **Make sure everyone knows the goals you are trying to achieve**—This will help you get everyone moving in the same direction.
- **Invest your time with your great employees to make them better**—Ted Winston has invested his share of time in people who in hindsight were never going to make it in his business. He now focuses on those who have the ability *and* the desire to take the organization to the next level.

The power of an engaged workforce can withstand any economic storm. Remember, these are the people who will do whatever it takes to exceed the expectations of both internal and external customers. Engaged workers will be the ones to innovate, rather than doing business as usual, which will help set your organization apart from the competition. While you may not have direct control over the high-level decisions being made at your firm, you will be glad to know that you have the power to drive employee engagement among your workers.

Studies have shown that the most important relationship an employee has is with his immediate supervisor. It's one of the top reasons that employees stay with their companies. And it's also high on the list of reasons employees choose to leave their jobs. It is also important to note that the things that attract people to a company may be very different from the things that keep them there or engage them. For example, compensation is usually a consideration in recruiting but will rarely be the reason that an employee will decide to stay with a firm. Sound leadership practices and solid relationships are what keep workers on the job and happily engaged, even at a time when companies are not able to increase wages as quickly as employees might like.

## The Road to Engagement

Towers Perrin, a leading global professional services firm, surveyed nearly 90,000 employees in eighteen countries, focusing on what drives attraction, retention, and engagement. Julie Gebauer, Towers Perrin's

managing director, provides an interesting perspective on the relationship between engagement and leadership. "Engagement is a two-way street, and companies are essentially the 'crossing guards' guiding which direction people move," observes Gebauer. The style of leadership you adopt will have a direct effect on which side of the road your employees wind up cruising down.

# Ways *You* Can Influence Employee Engagement

As evidenced by Barry Maher, there are lots of ways managers can personally affect employee engagement. According to the Towers Perrin study, the top behaviors that influence engagement include the following:

### EMPLOYEES FEEL THEY HAVE INPUT INTO THE DECISION MAKING IN THEIR DEPARTMENT

Do you ask employees for input prior to making changes that will have a direct impact on them? Do you usually discount what people say and do things your own way? Or are you known as someone who seeks the advice of those who are closest to the tasks at hand?

Most people want to do good work. You may not always think so, but for the most part, this is true. They also want to feel as if they have control over the work they do. If they don't feel this way, they'll simply do whatever they are told to do and nothing more. We see this a lot with young children, who usually have little control of how things will be done. If you ask a five-year-old child to pick up his toys he will do so, while stepping over the toys his sister has left on her latest tour of destruction. He's doing what he is told and nothing more. Is this the type of environment you want to set up for your people?

### EMPLOYEES FEEL THEY HAVE HAD THE OPPORTUNITY TO IMPROVE THEIR SKILLS AND CAPABILITIES OVER THE LAST YEAR

As a new manager, you probably feel pretty excited because you have likely had an opportunity to experience what it means to grow in your job. You've learned new skills over the past year and your capabilities have certainly improved, or your promotion would have gone to someone else. Now, don't you want members of your team to feel the

same way? Imagine what great things your team could accomplish together with this level of motivation.

When it comes to management, there is no one-size-fits-all approach. It's hard to know exactly what each employee needs in order to feel fulfilled. That's why it is helpful to ask members of your team what you can do to best support them. For some, this may mean granting permission to attend training courses and for others it may mean providing access to additional on-the-job training. Some members of your team may feel that you are willing to invest in them if you simply approve a request for reimbursement of trade books they purchased online or at the local bookstore.

## THERE IS A STRONG FEELING THAT MANAGEMENT IS SINCERELY INTERESTED IN AN EMPLOYEE'S WELL-BEING

You may think your employees should know you have their best interest in mind simply because that is what people in management should do. However, at some point in most people's careers, they've worked for someone who only has one thing on her agenda—her next move up the corporate ladder. These employees may have observed or even worked for people who continued to soar in their careers, with little consideration for their own people. Your employees have no way of knowing that your style is any different from what they've experienced until you demonstrate to them, as Barry Maher did, that you really do have their best interest in mind. That is why it is critical that your actions are congruent with your intentions.

Maher did this by taking the time to ask each of his employees about their short-term and long-term goals. He then made sure that when he asked for things, he highlighted the benefit to the employee. Taking the time to listen and understand how you can best support your employees, and then doing whatever it takes to help them achieve their goals, sends the message to your people that you have their interests in mind. Running interference on their behalf is another way to demonstrate that you have their back. Other ways to show your employees that you are fully committed to their success include encouraging them to continue their professional development, providing opportunities for them to stretch themselves in their jobs, and being willing to tell your boss that more work without more resources is simply not doable, given the circumstances.

# The Young, the Restless, and the Disengaged

I would be lying if I told you I sincerely believed you could get every disengaged employee to cross the road and walk on the right side. So what do you do with these people?

First, I'll tell you what you *don't* do with them, since this is a mistake that I see repeated over and over again. You don't ignore them, hoping they either change or quit. They may still be adding value to the organization; however, they are likely poisoning those around them. Most of us have been disenchanted with work at one point or another in our lives. We probably made sure everyone around us knew why we were so miserable. We didn't hesitate to talk about how lousy management was and complain about how poorly we were treated. And sometimes, if we were really angry, we let our customers know as well. We may not have done this intentionally, but our actions let customers and clients know that being there to serve them was the last thing we had on our mind.

Perhaps the only thing worse than disengaged employees are disengaged managers. If you find that you are working in an organization where the senior management team or the owner is obviously disengaged, then I suggest you find another job, as you will die on your sword trying to create an environment where people want to come to work every day.

For a moment, let's assume you have a team member who is disengaged. A disengaged employee no longer feels connected to her employer, and these feelings can be caused by things such as being passed over for promotion, finding out she is underpaid compared with others doing the same job, having a disagreement with a coworker or a member of management, losing trust in management, or the fear of possible change, such as a layoff or a merger.

The earlier you identify the signs of disengagement, the better chance you have of resolving issues and preventing further decay. Understanding how and why employees gradually lose their enthusiasm and begin to disengage can help us see how we, as managers, can salvage these relationships. Disengaged workers usually display a noticeable change in their behavior and attitude toward work and others. Here are five signs that an employee's connection to the organization may be weak.

1.  **A reliable employee is now less dependable**—The employee in question starts coming into work late or may suddenly begin to

use up sick days. Or, an employee who used to eat lunch at her desk every day begins to take extended lunches.

2. **An employee no longer contributes her opinions**—An employee who used to be quite vocal and was always willing to share her point of view now sits quietly in meetings, while others do most of the talking. When asked her opinion, she merely shrugs her shoulders.

3. **A valuable employee no longer volunteers to take on projects**—Suppose you have an employee who has a reputation of always asking for additional work. Suddenly, he is no longer volunteering to do so.

4. **A highly energetic team member who always did whatever was necessary to complete his work is now contributing at a minimal level.** This individual is doing as little as possible to receive a passing grade.

5. **An employee who used to participate in company functions no longer does.** This employee is trying to put distance between himself and his employer. He no longer wishes to feel connected with the people he works with.

Some of you may be in situations where, because you are managing people remotely, you may never actually see these signs. Or you might not be great at reading people yet, so you may be missing signs that a more experienced manager would easily recognize as a shift in behavior. So how can you prevent this from occurring? Sit down with or phone your direct reports on a regular basis and ask, "How is it going?" Then ask, "How are you feeling about things in general?"

Listen closely and pay particular attention to the tone they use when responding to you. Are their answers abrupt? Or are they willing to confide in you regarding issues that are weighing heavily on their minds? Have they provided you with an opportunity to begin a discussion that can eventually bring them back into the fold?

## Reconnecting with the Moderately Disengaged

When you have an employee whose work behavior has changed, or who you believe is becoming disengaged, there is no point in beating around the bush. Invite the person into your office for a private conversation regarding *your* observations. (Do not include hearsay or third-party observations in this conversation, as this will shift the con-

versation dramatically.) Begin by talking about the changes in behavior you have noticed and allow the employee time to speak freely. Refrain from passing judgment. Ask the employee what she feels she can do to deal with the problem and ask her what support she needs from you in order to do so. Encourage her by reminding her how valuable she is to the company—something she may have forgotten. Let her know what you are willing *and* able to do to support her as she gets back on track. Follow up periodically to ensure she continues to head in the right direction.

## Damaged Beyond Repair

There will be times when the relationship is too far gone to repair. No matter what you do, you will not be able to resuscitate this employee. So what should you do in situations like this? You must immediately cut this person out of your organization, before his negative attitude infects others. If you hesitate, it won't be long before you are spending the majority of your time trying to stop the outbreak of negative behavior that seems to have spread throughout your work group like a deadly virus in a sci-fi movie. This person must be managed out of the organization immediately, before he takes you and everyone else down too.

---
#### KEY LEARNING POINTS
---

- To succeed as a manager, you will need to shift your focus from "me" to "we." Going forward, your success will no longer be measured by your individual contribution to achieving the goals and objectives of your company. Instead, you will be evaluated on your ability to create and maintain a highly engaged team that is willing to give it their all.

- Employee engagement is defined as an intrinsic desire and passion for excellence, which feeds an employee's willingness to go above and beyond the call of duty. Research has shown time and time again that engaged employees are more productive and profitable, provide higher levels of customer service, and are less likely to leave when presented with a competitive offer from another company.

- As a manager, it is your job to be familiar with the signs that indicate an employee is less than engaged. These signs include

sudden changes in dependability, unwillingness to contribute opinions, lack of interest in taking on additional tasks and projects, contributing at a minimal level, and sudden refusal to participate in company functions.

- While difficult, it is certainly possible to bring a moderately disengaged person back into the fold. Ways to do this include demonstrating faith in the employee, meeting more frequently with the employee, providing continuous positive feedback, and demonstrating that you have the employee's best interest at heart.

- You can create a workplace where engagement flourishes by giving employees an opportunity to provide input into departmental decisions, making personal growth simply a part of the culture, assigning employees work that they find interesting and challenging, and showing you are sincerely interested in the well-being of your employees.

- You may encounter times when the CEO, owner, or executive team members are disengaged. If you are in this situation, the likelihood of you being able to create an engaged workplace for your people is quite low. Consider this before investing more time and energy into this organization, and don't be afraid to walk away if the forecast looks gloomy.

- You cannot fix everything or everyone. Highly disengaged employees are similar to a deadly virus. If you allow them to stay, they will infect others. Terminate these people, before it is too late.

---

*Purpose is at the base of everything we do. Our purpose at Virgin Hotels is, "Everyone leaves feeling better." Purpose sets the foundation for where you are going and where you are headed. We want our consumers to leave feeling better than when they arrive and wishing they could stay at the hotel a little longer, giving them more time to de-stress. The overall experience and the touch points of service are all aligned with our purpose.*

*Our purpose is also paramount to the way we interact with our teammates. We think about how their experience working here will leave them better than when they arrived. We also think, "Wouldn't it be great if when people had their tenure with us, they left thinking, 'Wow, they allowed me to be me. What a great experience I had working here.'"*

*Employee turnover in the hotel business is 60 percent, and we are at 30 percent. The guiding principle always, in everything we do, is our purpose. If you want everyone to leave feeling better, you have to have the process behind them working better.*

*Managers can build a purpose-driven department that is an example for all. Keep your purpose simple. You lead by your actions, so keep that in mind as you look to inspire others to unite behind your purpose.*

Raul Leal
*CEO*
*Virgin Hotels*

# Purpose: The Secret Ingredient that Will Separate You from the Pack

Think about the following scenario. You work for a boss who asks you to give more of yourself so the company can hit its financial numbers. (And by the way, "the company" happens to be your boss since he is the sole owner.) You slog into work and go through the motions of doing what's expected and nothing more. Now imagine working for a company and a leader whose express purpose is to improve the lives of your customers. You can't wait to arrive at the office and contribute your ideas, which your boss readily encourages.

I don't have to imagine what the first scenario is like, because I spent several years working for a financial services firm whose purpose was to make their wealthy clients *and* the founder wealthier. I had a difficult time fitting in, as I didn't see the firm's work as being very noble. You may view this as a noble purpose, in which case this environment may have worked as well for you as it did for my boss. She had no problem assimilating; she was all about the money and reminded us of this daily. I couldn't get out of there—and away from her—fast enough!

At its core, a company's purpose is a bold declaration of the reason a business exists. It conveys what the organization stands for, and it should drive everything you do. Employees today are seeking a deep connection to the work they do. They are looking for purpose. This is particularly true of Millennials, who want to make sure the time they spend doing something has value. There has to be meaning. As

a manager, it's your job to help your people connect the work they do with the overall purpose of the firm, as well as to their personal interest.

If you happen to be employed by a company that takes the opposite approach and begins every all-hands-on-deck meeting with statements like, "May I remind you that we are here to increase shareholder value?" don't despair. Later in this chapter, we'll discuss how to discover and ignite your team's purpose.

## Why Purpose Matters

I'm often asked why purpose matters, especially by Baby Boomers, many of whom have gone their entire lives without giving much thought to why they do the work they do. Here are some of the responses I give.

**Purpose provides people with clarity.** Have you ever worked in a job where you had no idea how your work fit into the mission of the organization? If so, you are not alone. There are lots of employees who come to the office and meander through their day. Let's make sure those people don't work for you. As a leader, it falls to you to make certain that organizational purpose is understood and carried out. Those with a clear sense of purpose are more likely to engage and be productive than those who are wandering through the organization like Bedouins looking for their next resting place.

**Purpose helps you attract the *right* people to your organization.** When you lead with purpose, you have a better sense of those who will fit in best with the culture of the organization. For example, suppose you work for a company like Pfizer, whose purpose is "Innovate to bring therapies to patients that significantly improve their lives." People who are satisfied with the status quo will be less likely to apply for work at Pfizer, which clearly requires innovation. Consequently, the hiring managers at Pfizer won't have to waste time sorting through resumes from people who aren't a good cultural fit. Those who are in alignment with your purpose will be the first in line to apply.

**Purpose inspires people to give it their best.** Purpose fuels passion. Take, for example, a pharmaceutical representative who refuses to quit work late on a Friday afternoon because she is saving lives. That kind of passion can only come from one thing: Purpose. Most likely, this representative works for a manager who frequently says, "Here's why we are here."

**Purpose increases employee satisfaction and productivity.** We all want a job that motivates and fulfills us. According to a recent study from LinkedIn and leadership training firm Imperative,[1] there is both an emotional gain and a fiscal gain that comes from finding purpose in your work. The results of the 2016 Workforce Purpose Index revealed that 73 percent of purpose-oriented workers reported being satisfied with their jobs compared to 64 percent of their non-purpose-oriented counterparts. And it's no secret that happier employees are more productive!

**Purpose increases employee retention.** Inspiring employees with a strong sense of mission and opportunities to work collaboratively toward a common goal creates the stickiness that keeps employees together. Today's workers are putting a premium on jobs that allow them to connect with their purpose. When employees find these opportunities, they are less likely to depart for what might appear to be greener pastures. The 2016 Workforce Purpose Index also revealed that 39 percent of purpose-oriented individuals are likely to stay with their employers three-plus years versus 35 percent of non-purpose-oriented professionals.

## How to Discover and Ignite Your Team's Purpose

Envision what it would be like if all of the members of your team were connected to purpose at work—to a job that mattered to them and their company. Imagine how much more productive and successful they'd be. Think of how much easier and more satisfying your job as a leader would be. Dreams do come true, and you don't have to work for Disney to make this so.

I mentioned that it's possible to create a sense of purpose for your team, even if your company isn't purpose driven. Here's an illustration of how this works. Suppose you manage accounts payable. In a traditional accounts payable environment, accounting clerks act more like defense players on a football team. They block and tackle and do whatever they can to keep vendors and department heads at bay. Or

---

[1] "2016 Workforce Purpose Index, Purpose at Work," Imperative and Linkedin, 2016, https://cdn.imperative.com/media/public/Global_Purpose_Index_2016.pdf.

at least it feels that way. Surely this can't be a very satisfying job for those in this role.

It doesn't have to be this way. You can create a sense of purpose for your team that aligns with the values you are trying to instill. Begin by answering the question, "Why does this team or department exist?" In this scenario, a common answer would be, "We exist to pay bills." Next, answer the question, "Who are our customers and what do they *really* need?" The answer is, "Department heads and vendors are our customers, and they need us to make bill paying easy." You can then create a purpose for your department that would sound something like,

> *"We are in the business of making life easier for department heads and vendors."*

The next step would be communicating the team purpose to your people, followed by a review of all accounts payable policies and procedures, with an eye toward making the lives of department heads and vendors easier.

# Four Important Characteristics of Your Work Group's Core Purpose

When creating your work group's core purpose, it's best to align your team with the company's purpose. In situations where there is no defined overall company purpose, keep the following in mind.

1. The core purpose must be easily understood. Too often people go overboard and the purpose gets lost in translation. Keep it simple.
2. People must be able to easily connect with the purpose. In the accounts payable example, most people would agree that having an easier life is something we can all strive for.
3. It must be something to which people are willing to dedicate their energy. Striving to better serve internal customers and improve relationships with external vendors is certainly something people can get behind as opposed to the monotonous task of paying bills.
4. It must feel meaningful. Empty slogans won't cut it. You'll know you've uncovered the essence of your team's core purpose when your people demonstrate a strong conviction and a deep feeling about their work.

# Three Questions Every Leader Must Ask about Purpose

If you believe your team exists solely to create products, deliver services, or make money, then you are missing a huge opportunity to fully engage the hearts and minds of your people. Purpose is the glue that holds your team together. Purpose guides and inspires people to work toward a common goal. Here are three questions to think about when developing your team's purpose.

1. **Why does our team or department exist?** Asking this question helps you gain clarity around what your team is there to accomplish.
2. **If our team disappeared tomorrow, what would be lost?** This question will help you uncover how vital the team is to the operation, and it will aid you as you look to align your department with the rest of the organization.
3. **Why would team members dedicate their time, effort, and commitment to our department?** Today's workers have plenty of options. What are you offering your team members that is so compelling? (Hint: The answer has nothing to do with compensation.)

# How to Lead On Purpose: The Seven Principles of Purposeful Leadership

Creating a team purpose statement is an important part of the purposeful leadership equation. However, the statement itself is a beginning, rather than a means to an end. Everything you do as a leader will be governed by the foundation you've just set for your team. Follow these seven principles of purposeful leadership and you will heighten the employee and customer experience.

## PRINCIPLE ONE: BE TRUE TO YOURSELF SO YOU CAN BE TRUE TO OTHERS

I know lots of leaders who keep trying to convince themselves that their work really matters. In some of these cases it may matter, but not to their current employer. You can't ask your people to believe in

something you don't believe in. For example, suppose you're disenchanted at work because you don't believe the company really cares about their people or customers. You have a choice. You can remain in place and attempt to change what no longer is working, or you can find another employer whose values more closely align with yours. What you shouldn't do is nothing.

This whole concept of purpose relies on consistent behavior that aligns with your overall commitment to your beliefs. It's not something you can demonstrate one day and ignore the next. The people on your team are watching your every move. They can tell when you are not fully invested. It's hard to fake enthusiasm and passion. Don't bother trying. It will backfire.

## PRINCIPLE TWO: TELL THE TRUTH WHEN NO ONE ELSE WILL

There will be times (okay, lots of times) when departmental practices are not serving the company's purpose or your department's purpose. Many new leaders might simply go with the flow for fear of what might happen if they challenge what is now the norm. You cannot let fear get the best of you or stop your people from speaking up when something no longer feels right. Take a stand and encourage your employees to do the same. Honesty pays.

Don't just go with the flow for the sake of peace and harmony. Voice your opinion in a respectful way so others are willing to entertain your ideas and suggestions. When appropriate, do this in the company of your people, so they can see firsthand that you mean business when it comes to being authentic.

## PRINCIPLE THREE: MANAGE FROM THE HEART AND CONNECT WITH PEOPLE'S SOULS

You are going to have to make some difficult decisions throughout your career as a manager. When doing so, I hope you will lead with your heart. Here's an example of how to do so.

I first started my career in Houston in the oilfield industry, which at the time was booming. We hit a slump in oil prices and lives changed overnight. Lots of people, including myself, had to deliver the news of layoffs to workers. I recall one manager who decided he was going to do whatever he could to preserve the livelihood of those with dependents. Rather than following the rules, he decided to change them. He knew that several people on his team were very marketable and could easily relocate. He offered them the choice of accepting a very generous

separation package or staying and possibly facing additional layoffs, with less lavish packages. One of the people who accepted his offer was a friend of mine. She grabbed the package, moved back East, was gainfully employed in no time, and started her new life with a nice nest egg in the bank. Others followed suit, which allowed the boss to save the jobs of those who weren't as mobile. I think of this manager from time to time and smile. He followed his heart and connected to the soul of his people in a way that made a huge difference for years to come.

## PRINCIPLE FOUR: LEAD WITH RESPECT

Respectful leadership begins with you. Managing with purpose requires the ability to command with respect. Giving orders as if you are managing a bunch of minions will do little to move your purpose forward. In fact, it will have the opposite effect. Some people will question your fitness to be a leader while others won't bother doing so. They'll simply pack their belongings and leave.

The golden rule of treating people as you'd like to be treated yourself is important when seeking to establish and maintain relationships with those you manage. Be mindful of your tone when giving directions. I wish someone had given me this advice, as I'm sure there were many times I was barking orders to my people when instead I should have been requesting their assistance.

## PRINCIPLE FIVE: KEEP YOUR BEHAVIOR IN LINE WITH YOUR INTENTIONS

When I began managing, I had noble intentions. I wanted to be the best boss anyone ever had. I failed miserably, as my behaviors were not in alignment with my intentions. Here's an example of how my wires got crossed. I wanted my team to feel empowered. Yet I managed to squash their ideas before they could finish their sentences. I didn't do this out of malice. I interrupted them in an attempt to quickly build upon what I thought they would say, so we could move the process along more rapidly. The end result was a team of discouraged workers. My behavior didn't exactly make it into the "best boss" category.

As you look at ways to lead with purpose, take stock of your behaviors to ensure they reflect your intentions and are representative of the example you are trying to set. If you use the example of the department purpose statement we created, "We are in the business of making life easier for department heads and vendors," but you insist on sending a department head back for additional approval signatures

that you could have obtained easily with a click of a button, then you are not living the purpose you've created. Your behaviors will be duly noted. Don't be surprised when you soon earn the reputation of the guy who gives lip service and nothing more.

## PRINCIPLE SIX: PROVIDE CLEAR DIRECTION SO OTHERS CAN FOLLOW

People really want to do a good job. Yet, the deck is stacked against them. Much of the letdowns I see are due to lack of clarity. You've got some managers who don't know where the heck they are going and others who are changing direction on a daily basis. For instance, I met the other day with a COO and his CHRO to discuss ways I could help support their management team. I immediately identified signs of dysfunctional behavior. In particular, the relatively new CEO was giving his key executives no clear direction. Both of these leaders were chomping at the bit to move forward, yet they were stuck in the mud waiting for the CEO to announce what direction the company was moving toward.

You have to be crystal clear on your vision for your team or department. Then you have to communicate this on a regular basis and inform team members when you foresee that a shift is about to occur.

## PRINCIPLE SEVEN: PROVIDE PURPOSEFUL RECOGNITION

I hate awards shows. The same people are recognized year after year, even if this year's performance is not worthy of recognition. Luckily, I can choose not to watch these shows. I see a similar occurrence at work. Recognition takes place on an annual basis, and oftentimes it's anything but authentic.

I believe organizations would be better served with purposeful recognition. This happens when you pay close attention and you catch your people doing something worth noting. Here's an example of what this looks like. Founder and CEO of Broughton Hotels, Larry Broughton, understands the importance of treating his team members the way he'd like his guests to be treated. "This is a relationship business," notes Broughton. "The way we treat our team members is how our team members treat our clients."

He believes leaders need to institutionalize their efforts to reward, recognize, and reinforce the behaviors they'd like their employees to continually display. They have to do this on purpose every day. He

explains, "We have a program called the Dollar Star Program. We want to catch people doing something right. We give each team member two origami stars made from dollar bills. When a team member is awarded an origami star, he in turn must give an origami star to a teammate. We do this because we want to encourage them to catch their team-mates doing something right."

Broughton Hotels has more than seven hundred employees, and it runs based on the premise that if you want to do great things, you have to be a great person. Broughton makes a point of working on this attitude daily, because he understands that the way his employees feel about their experience at work, and in turn the way they treat their guests, starts with him.

---

## KEY LEARNING POINTS

- A company's purpose is a bold declaration of the reason a business exists.

- A company's purpose conveys what the organization stands for, and it should drive everything you do.

- Employees today are seeking a deep connection to the work they do. They are looking for purpose. This is particularly true of Millennials, who want to make sure the time they spend doing something has value.

- Purpose provides people with clarity and helps you attract the *right* people to your organization. Purpose fuels passion and increases employee satisfaction and workplace productivity.

- If your company doesn't have a purpose statement, you can still create one for your team or department. Begin with the question, "Why does this team or department exist?" Follow this question with, "If our team disappeared tomorrow, what would be lost?" and, "Why would team members dedicate their time, effort, and commitment to our department?"

- Your core purpose statement must be easily understood, easy for people to connect with, and meaningful.

- Keep in mind the seven principles of purposeful leadership. Be true to yourself so you can be true to others; tell the truth when no one else will; manage from the heart and connect with people's souls; be a respectful leader; keep your behaviors in line with your intentions; provide clear direction; and offer purposeful recognition.

---

Finding top talent is a costly, time-consuming and risky business. In my experience top talent is a relatively scarce resource and the competition amongst employers to attract such people is huge. So the first thing that a manager who employs top talent needs to do is to understand what motivates them and make sure their needs are addressed.

There is a very clear business case for keeping top talent well paid as the cost and risk of a replacement can run into at least 5 figures—just think about the emotional and commercial damage which recruiting the wrong person can cause within a team.

But it is not all about money as most top talent is looking for job satisfaction and an environment that will give them the challenges they desire. To such a person their boss, and the way in which they are managed, is absolutely key. A good manager will delight in having someone working for them who is stronger than they are, and will understand how to inspire a strong team.

Chris Jones
*Director*
*The Display Centre (UK) Ltd*

# Talent Magnetism

*"The one thing that I wasn't prepared for when I was promoted into management was how to manage people who were not in sales," stated Joseph Lilly, former CEO of Seymour Consolidated Brands. "I didn't understand that people have different dispositions, which often varied depending on their role in the organization."*

Joseph Lilly's failure to recognize early on that certain traits are more beneficial than others, depending on the organization and position, made his entry into management a lot more difficult than it really had to be. It wasn't until years later, when Lilly brought in someone who specialized in managing operations, that he had this epiphany. Luckily for you, you don't have to wait years. You just have to read this chapter and you'll be well on your way to hiring for success.

Get your highlighters ready. Why? There is a lot of information here worth noting. When you choose your employees well, everything else will fall into place. You will eliminate the negative consequences of costly hiring mistakes, including low morale that can taint the fruits of your labor with just one bad apple in your bunch. You will be able to dramatically reduce the amount of energy you would normally expend on performance-related issues and instead have time to help your "A" players reach their *full* potential. Some of you may be thinking, "This all sounds great. All I have to do is read this chapter and I'm there!" If only life were that easy. There is much to learn about attracting and selecting talent. You may need to read this chapter more than once or my book, *Talent Magnetism* (Nicholas Brealey, 2013). You will need to practice these skills to become proficient. Be prepared to make some mistakes. It happens to the best of us!

# Talent Magnetism 101

When the first edition of *Suddenly in Charge* was published, the U.S. was coming out of one of the worst recessions in recent history. I advised managers to focus on mastering the skill of employee selection because there were significantly more unemployed people than jobs. A lot has changed since then. In many industries, there are considerably more jobs than qualified candidates. This situation is happening globally as well.

I woke up this morning to a Facebook message sent to me by a friend in Australia asking for my help. His company has over $100M worth of guaranteed sales and they are unable to service the business because they can't find skilled carpenters to do the work. I can't think of one of my clients who has not been impacted by today's labor market.

One of the most important skills you will need to master as a manager is the ability to attract and select top talent for your organization. Do this well, and you will spend significantly less time correcting problems and interviewing replacement candidates. Fail to master this skill and it may not be long before you find yourself on the other side of the interviewing desk.

We will begin with the basics to ensure you have a strong foundation to support your newly acquired skills. To do this, let's take a closer look at some of the most common mistakes made by hiring managers.

1.  **Only seeking talent when you have jobs to fill**—This is a rookie mistake even experienced managers make. Recruiting and hiring team members takes considerable effort. Think about it. The moment an employee gives notice, he's already checked out mentally. This means you're doing his job while still being responsible for your own work. You have to carve out time you don't have to find a replacement, while maintaining your department.

    Smart leaders are always looking for talent. The way to attract talent is to become known as the person people should speak to when considering their next career move. Here are some ways you can do this.

    - Meet with anyone who wants to discuss job opportunities with you, whether you have a job opening or not. Stay in touch with those who impress you. Reach out to them the moment a position becomes available.

    - Speak wherever you can, so you become known in your industry or community. This includes Rotary Clubs, Chamber of

Commerce meetings, local association meetings, conferences, and college clubs. If you do a good job, most likely audience members will approach you and ask if they can stay in touch.

- Take on a leadership role in your trade association. Those who do usually gain more exposure than people that simply join and occasionally show up for meetings.
- Build your LinkedIn network. Accept invitations from people in your field, even if you haven't personally met.
- Stay in touch with summer hires or interns. Send them an occasional email and be sure they are invited to the company holiday party.

2. **Failure to clearly define the role**—I often hear hiring managers say they will know it when they see it. My response is, "How will you know 'it' if you have no idea what 'it' is?" This approach reminds me of dating when you are sixteen years old. You see someone you are attracted to and you immediately think, this is the one. Never mind that the two of you have nothing in common. You just know it's going to work. Of course, few of us marry someone we dated in our teens. That's because at some point, we realize that it is going to take more than a hunch to guarantee there will be a happily-ever-after ending.

Before beginning the hiring process, clearly define the role your new employee will be filling. This is often referred to as writing a job description, although I prefer results descriptions where you list what is expected from anyone who is in this position. List *all* the duties and responsibilities this person will be given. You can always go back and shorten this list. Then take a look at the *minimum* skills and education required to do this job, and put this under the section we will call minimum qualifications. Notice how I said "minimum." Think about it. Although it might be nice to hire a marketing assistant with a Ph.D., is this really what you need and will someone with these credentials be happy in a position like this? Then review the description. Does it describe one position or three, which will be impossible to fill with just one person? Then go back and make any revisions so you are clear on what exactly you are looking for. I suggest doing this even if you work for a mom-and-pop organization where the concept of job descriptions may seem totally radical.

3. **Failure to cast a wide net**—Let's face it. Hiring is exhausting. Why not simply select from the best pool of candidates that are within your line of vision and be done with it? There are a number

of reasons why this approach may not yield the results you are seeking. Let's suppose you limit your decision to employee referrals. More than likely, you will wind up with a team that looks and thinks alike, as people usually hang out with those with whom they have a lot in common. Or suppose you decide to limit your job posting to a low-cost site like Craigslist. Will you miss out on exceptional candidates who may not be actively seeking new opportunities?

The cost of hiring has dropped considerably, thanks to the Internet and the explosion of social media. There are so many resources out there that it can feel overwhelming. Some are better than others. The wider you cast your net, the more likely you will find that perfect match. I remember when I lived in Boston and was searching for my perfect romantic match. I was very clear that I would not date anyone outside of the town in which I lived. Of course that was limiting, so I extended my parameters to include those within a thirty-mile radius. No great results to report. I then widened my reach again and still didn't find many viable candidates. It wasn't until I decided to cast my net as far as it would go that I met my perfect match. If only I had done that in the beginning, I would not have wasted countless hours trying to select the best of the worst from my limited pool, nor would I have used precious resources trying to transform the wrong candidates into something they were never going to become.

Today the place to search for candidates is LinkedIn. No doubt in the future there will be another "in place" on the web to find talent. It's important to stay abreast of talent trends. This will help to ensure you are in the right place at the right time.

Cast your net as wide as you can throw it. Hiring managers should leave no stone unturned. Use your social network and leverage the relationships you have developed through work-related associations or personal organizations. Think outside the box. Where might your potential candidates be hanging out? You would not believe the amount of networking that takes place on soccer fields all across the world, as parents watch their offspring try to become the next David Beckham!

4. **Refusal to pay recruitment fees**—Sometimes the person you need to hire may not be readily available, or you may simply not have the time to sift through a ton of resumes. This is where a recruitment agency, which gets paid only when they place a candidate, or a search firm, which is paid up front to go out and find exactly the type of employee you are looking for, can be

beneficial. The use of search firms is usually limited to companies that are hiring executives or extremely hard-to-fill positions.

When working with a third-party agency, you need to understand that they are working for *themselves*. The person who helps find candidates for your job opening will be paid a commission *only* if he makes a placement. It's a tough business, and it is not unusual to find that the person who helped you hire someone six months ago is no longer there the next time you call.

The best way to find a third-party agency to work with is through referrals, as there are some agencies that use practices that are less than ethical. For example, they may try to pluck the candidate they recently placed in your firm when they have a similar job order to fill six months later. Or, they may hold off sending you an average candidate until you've seen a few candidates you'd never hire. They hope you will find this average candidate exceptional, based on what you've already seen. When working with agencies, resist the temptation to whittle down the commission fees you pay to way below the average or the better candidates will go to the firm that is paying full freight, while you receive the leftovers.

5. **Hiring for skills, rather than fit**—If we go back to our dating example, we can probably think of a number of people we would have considered as life partners (or at least as second dates) based on a list of "qualifications" we may have written down. Yet we know that in many cases, formalizing these relationships would have ended in a disaster. That is because our values may not have been in alignment. Everyone comes to the table with certain traits (also known as behaviors or competencies) that we've either learned in the sandbox or are ingrained in our personalities. If you've ever tried to change the behavior of an adolescent, then you know how difficult (if not impossible) changing behavior can be. Try transforming a thirty-five-year-old employee who prefers to work in solitude into a team player. Can it be done? Maybe, but not without a lot of pain, and certainly the endeavor carries no guarantee of success. Why not hire someone who thrives off the energy of others, allowing the more introverted candidate to find a position in which the ability to stay focused for long periods of time and to work independently are highly valued?

6. **Settling: Hiring Mr. Right for right now**—So here you are. You've just been promoted, you're trying to learn your new job, and you are responsible for the work of others. In walks a candidate who can plug the hole that was created recently when your

best employee decided to go on a walkabout in Australia for the next year, and perhaps beyond. You do what most inexperienced managers do. You settle. You figure this guy will be adequate and you are right. He's adequate and nothing more.

Remember, you are only as good as the people on your team. Do you want to be known as the manager who is "adequate" or do you want to be the manager with the reputation for having an unbeatable team? If it's the latter (and if it's not, you might as well join that guy on his walkabout), then you must never settle. If you look long and hard enough, you will find exceptional employees. But you must believe this is possible and that you deserve this, or you will have a difficult time convincing these people that you are worthy of their talent.

Before making a final hiring decision, ask yourself the following questions:

- Have I seen enough candidates to know that this person is right for the position?
- Did I cast my net wide enough to ensure that I had an ample pool of qualified candidates from which to choose?
- Will this person help take our team to the next level?
- Do I have any concerns about this candidate that may indicate I am settling?
- Have I invested the time and energy that I need to invest in a proper search, or am I just ready to get this over with?

Once you've examined your responses to these questions, you will know whether you are making the best hiring decision possible given what you know or whether you are settling.

# The Case for Hiring on Talent, Rather than on Skills

I've always been a believer that you can train most people to do anything if they have certain traits that indicate they will be successful in the role. Of course, there are certain jobs, particularly those in the medical field, where skills will always trump behaviors. For example, if I were hiring physicians for a hospital, I would select surgeons who have demonstrated that they are at the top of their field over those who

have a pleasing personality but limited experience. The doc with the pleasing personality may have traits that indicate he would be a fast learner, but my feeling is, let him learn on someone else's time! We are talking about life and death here.

Fortunately most of the hiring you will do will not be a matter of life and death, although it certainly may feel that way to you. Experts agree that hiring for talent is the way to go. In their book *First, Break All the Rules*, authors Marcus Buckingham and Curt Coffman share findings from two massive studies conducted by the Gallup Organization over the last twenty-five years. These studies were conducted to determine what makes great managers great. The managers who became the focus of Gallup's research were invariably those who excelled at turning each employee's *talent* into performance. Buckingham and Coffman go on to explain how the best managers select an employee for talent rather than for skills or experience.

In the late 1990s, I was employed as an HR director for a transportation company. The company had 320 employees in eighteen locations, and I was running solo. To say that I was doing the job of two people would be an understatement. Eventually, I was given the go-ahead to add another person to my staff. There were many "qualified" candidates to choose from for this role, but few indicated that they possessed the talent needed to build a world-class human resource organization. That's when I met Megan. She was a recent liberal arts graduate who had moved to Boston to make her mark. And that she did!

Megan had absolutely no background in HR, nor had she worked in a business environment. But here's what she did have. Megan had been working since the age of fourteen. She had an entrepreneurial spirit that wouldn't quit and had started a few small businesses before she left for college. She came from a family of means, although you would never know it. (She lived in an apartment with two other women in order to make it on her own.) She was smart, self-motivated, and willing to do whatever it took for us to meet our crazy goals. I hired her for her potential, and when I left the organization five years later she was well equipped to take on my role, which is exactly what she did. That's what you call hiring for talent.

Most stories don't have happy endings like Megan's because hiring managers find people who've done the job before and assume they've found the perfect match. Yes, they may have been the perfect match, but for someone else. Their values may have aligned with those of the organization they recently left but may be the opposite of what fits into your organization. This would explain why a candidate who

was successful in his last job can turn out to be a disaster when he works somewhere else. The honeymoon period ends quickly when the manager realizes that some things, like attention to detail, passion, and assertiveness, simply cannot be taught.

When hiring, consider future needs, rather than staffing for what is needed today. Find your own Megan and make her an offer.


## Speed Trumps Perfection

Managers are taking way too long to hire and are losing out on great talent. Candidates are in hot demand these days. Many are receiving multiple job offers from other employers on their mobile devices as they are leaving your office. Here's how you can dramatically reduce your time to hire.

- Make a list of everyone involved in the hiring process. Draw a line halfway through the list. The people below the line will no longer be involved in the hiring process.
- Phone screen candidates. At first glance, this may appear to add time to the hiring process. I can assure you it won't. One brief phone interview and you'll have a good sense if a candidate is worth further consideration. Many won't make it through the phone screen, which will free you up so you can move qualified candidates through the process without delay.
- Conduct reference checks on your top two candidates before their last interview. In doing so, you may find out only one candidate is worth a final look.
- Work with your boss or HR to assemble a job offer you can extend on the spot.


## Changing Behavior

Some people may argue that of course you can change behavior. They will then cite examples of people they have been able to change. But at what cost? Perhaps after years of therapy (and dollars) they have been able to get their spouse or child to change their behavior. Or maybe

they were able to transform an employee who perhaps needed a bit more TLC to reach their potential. Was that really a behavior change?

I would argue that yes, some behavior can be changed. But why would you try to square a circle when there are plenty of circles out there that will fit right into your organization? Most inexperienced managers do not possess the skills needed to create behavior changes. Perhaps you will develop these abilities with time, but right now this is the last thing you should be doing. Remember, your job is to help your "A" players soar. Can you really do this if you are spending half your day working with people who may not have the raw materials necessary (or the desire) for you to mold them into a work of art?

In the next chapter we will dive into how to determine which candidates possess the traits and talent that will be the right match for your situation.

---

## KEY LEARNING POINTS

- It's easier to attract talent than it is to recruit employees. As a leader you should always be looking for talent. The way to attract talent is to be known as *the* person people should speak to when considering their next career move. Speak wherever you can, get involved in industry associations, and be willing to meet with anyone who is interested in learning more about your organization.

- One of the most important skills you will need to master is the ability to select top talent for your organization. Do this well, and you will be able to focus your time on developing a team that is aligned with the goals and values of the organization. Fail to master this skill and you will waste countless hours correcting performance-related problems and interviewing replacements.

- Don't even think about beginning the selection process until you have taken the time to clearly define the position. This way you won't waste time assessing candidates who should never have been brought in for an interview in the first place.

- Hire for fit and talent; train for skill. If you hire someone who is inquisitive, a quick learner, and interested in taking on new challenges, she should have no problem learning what she needs to know to be successful on the job.

- Companies are taking way too long to hire, and as a result they are losing out on talent. Examine your hiring process and look for ways to collapse the interviewing cycle. Be ready to make an offer to your top candidate the moment you know this person is the one.

---

*Retention is personal: If a firm is worried about retaining staff (and they should be if replacing talent is difficult and expensive), they often take a top-down approach. For instance, they'll give retention bonuses or offer a perk like free chair massages on Fridays.*

*The problem is that retention is highly personal. Why employee A stays (perhaps the ability to learn and grow) might be wildly different from employee B's reason (the stability and generous medical benefits). While it seems inefficient, it is highly effective to manage retention on a 1:1 basis, creating a unique strategy for each employee whom you desire to retain.*

*It's also important to keep in mind that some attrition is healthy: When staff quit it can sting the manager and be a sense of loss for the team, in addition to the ego hit. However, if the employee was an average or underperformer you just created a spot for a high achiever.*

Ben Brooks
*CEO*
*PILOT*

# Guard Your Exits: How to Prevent Your Employees from Taking the Next Flight Out

N obody likes to talk about it, even though it is happening in workplaces all across America: Employees who have decided it is time to fly the coop. Departure lounges are overflowing with these types of employees—all waiting for their final boarding call.

## Common Reasons Employees Leave Their Job

Employees rarely start a job thinking they will tour around the company for a while and then seek greener pastures, and yet it happens all the time. Here are some of the more common reasons why people are departing in droves.

### THEY DON'T LIKE THEIR BOSS

Studies consistently show that employees don't leave companies. They leave their managers. I know this was true for me and most likely for some of you. If you apply the advice I'm providing you in this book, you won't experience firsthand what it's like for an employee to leave because of you. If this has already happened, it's good to examine what transpired so you can avoid making the same mistakes twice.

Before you begin to rate your performance as a leader, it's important to understand that sometimes people don't see us as we see ourselves. A survey of managers and employees in workplaces throughout the United Kingdom, conducted by HR consultancy Penna,[1] revealed that managers rank their own performance more highly than do their direct reports. In fact, their research found that more than half of employees went so far as to say they could do a better job than their manager.

Among the behaviors employees disdain about their boss are

- Micromanagement
- Dishonesty
- Favoritism
- Poor communication
- Indifference
- Taking credit for others' ideas
- Lack of recognition
- Little follow-through
- Lack of management support

Don't be dismayed after reading this list. Knowledge is power. Now that you know what turns people off about their leaders, you can focus on being the type of leader whom people *really* enjoying working with.

## THE HIRING PROCESS IS FLAWED

Are employees exiting as quickly as you are hiring them? If this is the case, then there is a malfunction in your hiring system. Closely examine all the parts of your hiring process to determine which pieces must be fixed. For example, suppose turnover is particularly high during the first ninety days of service. Ask yourself the following questions.

- *Am I hiring the right types of people for these jobs?* Yes, it is nice to hire Ivy League graduates, but are they really well suited for beverage sales?

---

[1] Jo Faragher, "Managers Have Higher Opinions of Themselves Than Their Teams Have," *Personnel Today*, March 2016.

- *Am I accurately representing job openings to candidates?* If your administrative job description sounds more like the CEO's job, then it is time for another rewrite.
- *Do I overpromise and underdeliver?* Perhaps it is time to get real. Sure, in our dreams our organization closely resembles Google, but few companies actually do. Accurately describe your work environment and let candidates decide if the fit is right for them.

## THEY FEEL NO CONNECTION TO THEIR MANAGER

In today's work environment, it's not uncommon for workers to report to someone who is located in a different part of the country or in some cases a different country. You would think that communication between managers and their team members would be stronger given all the technology we have at our fingertips. Sadly, this is not the case. Managers are using apps like Snapchat to communicate with their people, and many rely heavily on texting. While I'm all for brevity, I also believe there is a time and place for meaningful conversations.

It's a heck of a lot easier to depart when you feel no connection to the person you are working for. It's up to you, the leader, to create a solid, meaningful relationship with your people. Here are some ways to do this:

- If you work in the same building, think twice before sending an email or text to your employee. Instead, walk down to this person's cubicle and have a face-to-face conversation.
- If your employee works remotely, use Skype.
- Make it a point to check in weekly with team members and ask them how it's going.
- Get to know your people on a personal level. I'm not suggesting you check in regarding how their date went last night. However, questions like, "How's that graduate class going?" or, "Has your son settled on a college yet?" would certainly be welcome, particularly if you follow it up with something like, "Let me know if I can be of help!" This approach will demonstrate that you are interested in more than just productivity.

## THEY DON'T SEE OPPORTUNITIES FOR
## PROMOTION OR GROWTH

No one grows up saying, "When I grow up I want to be in a dead-end job." Yet so many people find themselves in this very same position. When the economy is strong, people have more choices. If you don't give them an opportunity to grow, someone else will.

Those of you working in larger organizations with more resources certainly have the upper hand here. But that doesn't mean if you're a manager in a smaller organization, you're out of luck. Here are some ideas you can apply, regardless of company size, to support the growth of your people:

*Develop an individual growth plan with each employee.* Don't assume an employee wants to pursue the same track that's gotten you where you are today. Having a conversation early on in an employee's tenure will provide you with a good sense of where that person would like to head. Together you can develop a plan that will help move the employee closer to those goals.

*Support your employees' continued education.* You may not be able to reimburse employees for classes they are taking to improve their skills, but you can certainly adjust their work schedule to ensure they can make it to class on time. You can also go to bat for them and try to get a one-day seminar approved, or at a minimum, reimbursement for a book that will help them gain new skills.

*Act as a mentor.* Bring a few employees to a customer meeting or have them present to the executive team the next time you are presenting your group's findings. You can also encourage them to get involved in a local trade association where they will be exposed to new ideas. If possible, offer to reimburse them for their membership and associated fees. If that's not plausible, consider bringing them as your guest the next time you attend a business function.

*Set up coaching.* If you have people on your team who are high potentials, consider hiring a coach so they can achieve their full potential. Group coaching is also another option that signals to your employees you are in it for the long run and hope they are as well.

# Signs Your Employees May Be Seeking Greener Pastures and How You Can Bring Them Back into the Fold

I can tell you exactly who in my network has recently begun to look for work. How? Their LinkedIn connections go from a total of fifty connections to fifty new connections a day! I also start receiving notifications indicating there's been a change in their LinkedIn profile.

It's not uncommon today for managers to connect with their staff via LinkedIn. If you're not connected, I'd strongly encourage you to send an invitation to connect today. I'm not suggesting this so you can spy on your people and call them out when you see suspicious behavior on their account. It's so you can have a pulse of what's going on with your team. If you see patterns like the ones I described, you'll know you need to pay immediate attention to particular employees. This may mean taking them out for a cup of coffee to discuss what could potentially be their next move in the company or to see what improvements you can make to increase their employee satisfaction.

Another sign is a sudden and frequent change in lunch plans. If employees start leaving the building for long lunches when they always used to eat quickly at their desk, something is probably up. Similarly, a sudden uptick in requests for Personal Time Off days may actually be a cover for outside interviews. An employee who is job hunting may begin to make private calls from the conference room.

New research conducted by CEB, a Washington-based best-practice insight and technology company, looks only at why workers quit but also at *when*. In a *Harvard Business Review* article titled "Why People Quit Their Jobs,"[2] Brian Kopp, head of CEB's HR practice, is quoted as saying, "We've learned that what really affects people is their sense of how they're doing compared with other people in their peer group, or with where they thought they would be at a certain point in life. We've learned to focus on moments that allow people to make these comparisons."

Employees tend to take stock of their careers on their birthdays, particularly midlife milestones such as turning forty or fifty; on work anniversaries (whether joining the company or moving into the current role); or when attending large social gatherings such as high school or

---

[2] "Why People Quit Their Jobs," *Harvard Business Review*, September 2016, pp. 20–21, https://hbr.org/2016/09/why-people-quit-their-jobs.

college reunions. These events are natural times for reflection. You may not know when people are about to head off to a school reunion, and you may not be aware they are about to celebrate a milestone birthday, but you can certainly take note of their work anniversary. Make it a point to have check-in conversations with your people several weeks prior to their anniversary date. Ask if they find their work challenging and interesting. Do they see a clear path as to their next move in the organization? These kinds of conversations can give you time to intervene and demonstrate to your employees that the best opportunity for career growth may be the one right in front of them.

## How to Pinpoint the *Real* Reason People Are Leaving

Imagine spending countless hours and tons of money trying to solve a problem, which in the end isn't really the problem. All the while, the problem still persists. For instance, a while ago I was asked to work with a major beverage company to help them improve their employee retention. They had calculated that they were losing millions of dollars a year due to their salespeople leaving the company within a year of their arrival. I told them that in order for them to get my help, I'd have to determine what problem we were dealing with. Luckily for them, they agreed.

This company did *not* have an employee retention problem. They had a hiring problem. Here's an example of what transpired. The company was recruiting salespeople at top-name universities and were then surprised when these employees gave notice to attend medical or law school. Their college recruiting program focused on institutions located in urban settings, even though 50 percent of their entry-level sales jobs were located in rural areas. It's no wonder why new hires were leaving in droves! They were never a good fit in the first place. If I hadn't uncovered this, they'd still be losing millions of dollars annually and would be no further along today than when they reached out to me for help.

The lesson here is to do your due diligence—or hire someone who can do so without bias—before attempting to solve what may turn out to be symptoms, rather than the real problem. I'm happy to report my client made many of the changes I recommended, including revising their targets for college recruiting, and within one year's time, employee turnover in their sales force was slashed in half.

# What to Do if People Are Leaving Because of You

I began this chapter by talking about people leaving their bosses. Given the frequency as to how often this occurs, I'd be remiss if I didn't cover what to do if people are leaving because of you.

Let's start by discussing what you *don't* want to do. In all likelihood, someone from HR will share the results from the exit interview they've just conducted with your departing employee, who may have said some less-than-flattering things about you. Naturally your first inclination might be to go on the defense and respond with, "What *exactly* did he say about me?" Don't take the bait. Listen to what's been said. Is there some truth to what the employee has shared with HR? Were there extenuating circumstances that the employee forgot to present? In these situations, the best thing to do is to ask for time to reflect on the feedback you've been given. This will enable you to prepare an appropriate response, if one is required.

You also don't want to seek out your current employees so you can conduct an investigation, like the ones you watch on your favorite criminal television show, to see if they feel the same as the person who is leaving. Chances are there is some truth in what's been said.

I recommend you think about what you are willing to do differently as a result of the feedback you've just received. In some cases, an apology may be in order. I know that if I had received feedback regarding how hard I was driving my people when I was their manager, I would have pulled my team together and apologized for being completely insensitive to the fact that even though I had no life outside of work, they did. I would have then asked for a volunteer to call me out on my behavior whenever I slipped back into my old habits. An apology can go a long way, but only if you mean what you say and are committed to making changes in the future.

It's hard for most people to change behavior. That's why I suggest you seek help. Some people join support groups or work with someone on an individual basis for self-improvement. You can do the same. See if someone in HR is willing to coach you so you can smooth some of the rough edges that may be causing harm to others. Ask if your company would be willing to provide you with a coach. If not, consider making the investment and doing so on your own. Whenever I coach people, the one thing they always say is that they wish they had engaged a coach years earlier. You have the chance to do so today. Don't delay.

# How to Create a Magnetic Connection with Your People

In my most recent book, *The Magnetic Leader: How Irresistible Leaders Attract Talent, Customers, and Profits*,[3] I write about magnetic leaders: People whose leadership style is irresistible, who have incredible connections with the people they serve, and who are the envy of many. These leaders don't stress out about losing great employees or good customers, because this rarely happens. Granted, it may feel like some people are born with the magnetic gene, but there's no reason to despair; magnetism can most certainly be taught.

## WHAT PEOPLE REALLY SEEK FROM THEIR LEADERS

Lots of leaders think they are magnetic when they are anything but. While researching *The Magnetic Leader*, I spoke to more than a dozen leaders whom I consider to be magnetic. I asked if they would be willing to share the secret recipe for magnetism. Here are four of the ingredients that go into the making of a magnetic leadership. For the rest, you'll have to read *The Magnetic Leader*.

### Authenticity

When I asked, "What makes someone a magnetic leader?" the word *authenticity* was usually the first word that came to mind among those I interviewed for my book. Magnetic leaders don't try to be someone they are not; nor do they change who they are based on office politics. They are true to themselves and are honest in their dealings with others. They are not afraid to share their mistakes or shortcomings. For example, Warren Buffett is an authentic leader who speaks openly about his $200 billion mistake buying Berkshire Hathaway.

Employees aren't seeking perfection from their bosses, yet leaders make efforts to hide their shortcomings. Admitting you're wrong every now and again and sharing your hopes as well as your fears will allow others to see you as human, rather than as your office's version of the horrible boss, Mr. Harkins (played by Kevin Spacey), from the movie *Horrible Bosses*.[4]

---

[3] Roberta Matuson, *The Magnetic Leader: How Irresistible Leaders Attract Talent, Customers, and Profits* (New York: Taylor and Frances, 2017).

[4] *Horrible Bosses*, July 8, 2011, New Line Cinema.

## Transparency

Leaders who are transparent are *consistently* honest and open in their communication—so much so that people never have to guess what these leaders really mean when they say something. This level of openness often spreads to the wider company culture. Tony Hsieh, CEO of Zappos, is the first person who comes to mind when I think of transparent leaders. From the very beginning, before blogs became all the rage, Hsieh would share openly the happenings (both the good and the bad) at Zappos for both employees and customers to see. In fact, the company's all-staff meetings were broadcast on the Internet.

On a scale of 1 to 10 with 10 being high, how would you rate your transparency? If it took more than a few seconds for you to respond, then the answer is "not high enough." Imagine working for a leader who tells you partial truths. Would you trust this person? Would you put your neck on the line for her? Probably not. No doubt there are times when you are unable to be completely transparent, such as disclosing conversations that the management team is having regarding a reduction in the workforce, but that doesn't mean you shouldn't tell an employee that this might not be the best time to buy a dream home. If the employee probes further, explain that this is all you are currently able to say.

## Continuous Feedback

I was having a conversation the other day with a magnetic CEO on the subject of feedback. He was saying, and I agree, that a strong leader provides a constant stream of feedback and does so even if the information he is sharing may not be what the other person is expecting. He told me about a time he had to tell an employee whom he had just started managing why he didn't get a promotion. Although it was hard to hear, the employee thanked him for his honesty and said this was the first time anyone had ever told him that. This gesture is how one goes about building magnetism. This CEO was authentic, he was transparent, and he provided feedback that his employee could use to improve his lot in life. Bravo!

In a recent survey conducted by global consultant leader Mercer titled "Employee Views on Moving Up vs. Moving On,"[5] the results

---

[5] "One in Three Employees Claim to Have a Job Rather than a Career, New Mercer Survey Finds," Mercer, August 2015, www.mercer.com/newsroom/one-in-three-employees-claim-to-have-a-job-rather-than-a-career-new-mercer-survey-finds.html.

revealed that more than half of employees (51 percent) report they receive "no input" or "input only once in a while" from superiors on how to perform better in their roles. See how easy it is to stand out from the crowd?

You don't have to set an alarm on your smartphone to remind you to provide continuous feedback. When you see team members doing a good job, tell them so. When you believe you'd be remiss if you didn't let an employee know his work isn't up to your expectations, then have that conversation. Don't wait until it gets to the point where you are praying every night that he'll resign so you won't have to tell him what really needs to be said.

## Career Development

Have you ever worked for a boss who put your career development before hers? Me neither. Career development wasn't that big a deal when I was coming up through the ranks—probably because we had formal management training programs. If you weren't invited to participate, you knew you weren't going any further.

Life is different today. As competition for talent heats up, companies are prioritizing employees' career development as a low-cost way to keep them around. At the same time, companies are struggling with managers' lack of transparency about career progression, which is impacting employee loyalty and is having a negative impact on employee retention.

Having conversations about career progression takes considerable time and effort. However, if you stop viewing career conversations as one more thing to add to your full plate, you might find you actually enjoy helping others achieve their goals and dreams.

Begin by asking your employee where she'd like to be in a year's time. Then extend this by a few years so together you can create a plan that will get her to where she wants to be. Approach your HR representative with an eye toward learning what internal resources may be available to your direct reports.

# The Leaving Speech: Why You Should Say Goodbye to Your Employees on the Day They Start

All managers should say goodbye to their employees on or near their first day of employment. You probably think I'm kidding. I'm not. My colleague Rob Nixon, CEO of PANALITIX, wrote a Facebook post one day that took my breath away. I asked him if I could share it with others and he readily agreed. Nixon was a guy who told me that he had twenty-five people quit in one year in his company and he only had fifteen positions. He realized he had a problem and that the problem was him. He took a hard look inside himself and became very clear about what he wanted his legacy to be and what he wanted his employees to experience. Here's his post, which he calls "The Leaving Speech."

Today marks the end of a five-years-and-two-months era. But it's also the start of a new one. One of our star performers, Sharon McClafferty, is leaving to look for new opportunities. She started as a sales coordinator and was quickly promoted into a sales role where she quickly started outselling seasoned professionals. Within twelve months she was the sales manager where she grew and led a team of seven people. She had never sold anything before joining our company yet in five years she has sold in excess of $5 million of new revenue. An absolute superstar. When Sharon sells she doesn't sell. That's the difference. She is an amazing relationship builder who makes a difference to those that she engages. She tells me she has done over 750 consultations to accountants, which is awesome.

On or close to the day she started I had the "leaving speech" with her. It went something like this.

"Sharon, welcome to the team. We're thrilled you're here. I am sure you're the right person for the job and I know there is a lot going on this week. I just wanted to talk to you for a few minutes about the day you leave. You will leave one day; everyone does. I know this is your first day and I know you'll leave sometime in the future so I figured we should talk about it now. I have a number of hopes and desires for that inevitable day. Firstly, I hope we part on good company. I don't want someone to fire you because you didn't work out or make you redundant because of a business downturn. Secondly, I hope that you learn a lot, contribute a lot, and have a lot of fun. Thirdly, I hope that you live by our values, service, and culture standards, and the standards we set become part of your

life. And lastly, when you look back at this block of time, no matter how long it is, you look back on it fondly as an amazing part of your career. Welcome to the team. That's all I wanted to say."

I do this with every new team member close to the day they start. Sharon has ticked all those boxes and she has grown into an extraordinary professional.

## How to Write a Leaving Speech that Will Get People to Stay

I advise all my clients to compose their own leaving speech, and I suggest you do the same. When doing so, speak from your heart. Here are some questions to get you started.

- What possibilities and dreams do you have for your people?
- How will they be better off having known you?
- What would you like them to say about their experience working for you?

Now imagine being a new employee and hearing a speech like Nixon's. If you're like me, you are probably thinking you're *finally* working for someone who is genuinely concerned about what you experience under his direction. It doesn't get much better than that. I doubt many people will be looking to jump ship when they have a leader who is deeply committed to making sure their last day is as fulfilling as their first day, and that every day in between is just as meaningful.

## Stay Interviews

Many companies rely on information gathered from exit interviews to improve their retention rates. The fatal flaw in this strategy is that exit interviews are reactive. They take place *after* the employee has made her decision to leave.

Stay interviews are done while the employee is still in your employ; these meetings are preventative in nature. Think of these interviews as a conversation between you and your people. You are trying to ascertain how likely they are to remain with your organization and

determine what areas you can improve upon in order to retain their commitment.

You don't have to conduct these interviews one-on-one, which is a good thing for those of you who are managing large work groups. Managers who have been most successful with this approach to employee retention are the ones who consistently demonstrate that they are willing and able to make changes based on what's been reported. It's also important to report back on those areas where you are unable or unwilling to address particular issues. This way, employees don't feel their comments have fallen into some black hole.

## Questions All Leaders Should Be Asking Their People on a Regular Basis

I like to keep things simple, and I'd encourage you to do the same. Here are some questions you should be asking your people on a regular basis.

1. How are things going?
2. What else do you need from me to be successful in your job?
3. How likely are you to recommend my work group or our company to others?
4. Where would you like to go next in the company, and how can I best support you in your endeavor?

## Drop the Excess Baggage

Remember when you were a kid on the playground in elementary school and you were standing on the sidelines hoping and praying to be chosen by the team with all the star players? Not much has changed since then. Great employees want to work with other great employees. They don't want to be picking up the slack from those who are barely limping along.

Now's the time to evaluate your team and to take action on some decisions you probably should have made months ago. If you want to keep your best people from leaving, you've got to give them a good reason to stay. Working with an all-star team is an awesome reason to

stay. Now's the time to drop the excess baggage that is weighing down your work group. Do this today.

──────────────── KEY LEARNING POINTS ────────────────

- Employees rarely start a job thinking they will tour around the company for a while and then seek greener pastures. They leave for a number of reasons, including the fact that they don't like their boss and they see little opportunity for promotion or growth.

- There are a number of signs that employees may be seeking greener pastures. Among these are a sudden uptick in the number of connections they are making on sites like LinkedIn, extended lunches, and an increase in phone conversations made or received in conference rooms. Recognizing the signs will help you bring them back into the fold before they are gone forever.

- Sometimes people are leaving because of you. Listen carefully to the feedback you are receiving. If you hear it more than once, most likely it's true. Find an internal or external coach to help you smooth some of your prickly edges that may be causing harm to others.

- If you want your people to stick around, then consider doing the work that is necessary to become a magnetic leader. Work on being authentic, being transparent, giving feedback continuously, and providing career development opportunities for those in your employ.

- People will remain deeply committed to leaders who want to be sure their last day is as fulfilling as their first day, and that every day in between is just as meaningful. Creating your own leaving speech will help to ensure the experience you intended for your people is the one they actually experience.

- Replace exit interviews with stay interviews.

- Touch base with your people on a regular basis and ask them how things are going, what you can do to help them be more successful in their job, if they are likely to recommend your work group to others, and how you can best support them as they look to progress in their career.

- Rid your team of low performers who are weighing your work group down. By doing so, you'll have an all-star team that few will want to leave.

*At age twenty-three, I became responsible for supervising a staff of direct reports. In my role at the time as a manufacturing supervisor for Merck, many of my reports were older than I. In fact, almost 50 percent of them have kids older than me!*

*Today when leading teams, I am constantly looking to build a culture of teamwork and company pride toward a common mission. When the team is working as one unit, employee-manager relations are at a high and everyone is winning!*

Mike Alston Jr.
*Associate Director*
*Sterogene Bioseparations*

# Generation Integration

## Leveraging Workplace Differences into Opportunities

I s it just me, or do the faces in the workplace look different these days? For the first time in history, we have four (or five, depending on who is counting) generations in the workplace. That is quite a change from the 1950s, when 60 percent of the workforce consisted of white males. These men were typically the sole breadwinners in the household, and they expected to retire by age sixty-five to spend their golden years on the golf course. What a difference a half-century makes!

Today, some workers don't even get their careers started until they are well into their forties. Some mature workers are returning to the workplace after raising families, while others are shifting gears either voluntarily (time to try something new) or involuntarily (their jobs have been shipped overseas). Thanks to the recession of 2009, older Baby Boomers (born between 1946 and 1964) delayed retirement as they try to rebuild their retirement portfolios. That left us with frustrated Gen Xers (born between 1965 and 1979), who thought they'd be moving into those corner offices, and, in the United States, with a slew of about 75.4 million younger workers, also known as Millennials (born between 1980 and 1992), who are challenging the way work is done on a daily basis. As if things weren't crazy already, we can now

add Gen Z (demographers place its beginning anywhere from the early 1990s to the mid-2000s) to the mix. (More on Gen Z and Millennial contributions later.)

As if management wasn't challenging enough, today's manager must be adept at leveraging generational workforce differences into opportunities. In order to do this, you must first understand where people are coming from, so you can better understand where they are headed and how to best manage them.

# Meet the Generations

By closely examining the differences and commonalities of each of the generations, you will be better prepared to unite your workforce. Let's begin by meeting the generations.

Of course, not everyone in each of the generations is like the characters in the following descriptions, but you can get a fairly good picture of each of the generations by reading their stories. Some of you may be thinking that you cannot relate at all to the person who represents your generation. That may be because you are on the tail end of one of these demographics. If you are on the cusp of one of the generations, you may better relate to the generation that is either before or after yours. But certainly we all know people who can easily fit into these descriptions.

### THE TRADITIONALIST (BORN BEFORE 1945)

Meet Max, Mr. Traditionalist. Max, who is now in senior management, grew up in the shadows of the Great Depression and has always been grateful to have a job. He started with the company thirty-five years ago in the mailroom and has remained loyal ever since.

Max is slowly adjusting to technology. He is able to e-mail pictures of his grandchildren to anyone in the office who might want to see them, but struggles sending e-mail attachments at work. This puzzles some of the younger workers, who are constantly called in to assist Max on technology matters.

Over the years, Max has put money away for his "golden years." Unfortunately, what Max and others in his generation couldn't foresee was the stock market tanking just before his scheduled retirement date. Max's portfolio has finally bounced back. He's now starting to think

about vacating his nice corner office. His younger coworkers wish he'd take time to enjoy the fruits of his labor while he still can. It's no secret that a few of them are in the break room plotting for his office.

## THE BABY BOOMER (BORN BETWEEN 1946 AND 1964)

Meet Barbara the Baby Boomer. She takes her work seriously (some may say too seriously). Barbara is thrilled to be a member of the first generation of women who were able to choose to work or stay at home.

Those who know Barbara well would describe her as competitive. She has competed with the millions of other Baby Boomers her whole life, all of whom were vying for a limited number of jobs.

Like many Boomers, Barbara tries to do it all. She works crazy hours while caring for her family and aging parents. Barbara thinks the younger workers in the firm are in awe of her ability to do it all, when in fact most wonder why someone would give everything they have to an organization that could easily let them go tomorrow.

## THE GEN XER (BORN BETWEEN 1965 AND 1981)

Michael is of Generation X, also known as Gen X. He is a fairly casual guy, and at first glance, you'd never guess he was a member of management, based on his informal attire. Michael doesn't see the value of spending disposable income on dry cleaning bills. After all, how many people come to visit him in his cube?

Michael is the kind of guy who likes to get things done. He doesn't understand the need for Boomers to call a meeting to talk about a meeting. He'd rather get the work done on his terms, which means he's rarely in the office before 9:00 A.M. or after 5:00 P.M.

Michael's workspace is sparsely decorated, so he can easily pack up his office at a moment's notice. You see, Michael grew up in a time of corporate downsizing. His dad was laid off more times than Michael can remember. He knows that no job is forever.

## THE MILLENNIAL (BORN BETWEEN 1982 AND 2000)

Meet Ashley. She's young, she's hip, and she's ready to launch her career in marketing . . . as soon as she's finished downloading a hot new song to her smartphone . . . on company time.

People in Ashley's generation have grown up in an environment where their parents have done it all for them, and in some cases are

still doing it all for them. She asks a lot of questions, and when she forgets, her mother steps in!

Like her peers, Ashley is accustomed to multitasking. She's a techno wiz and can type faster than most people in the office, yet she can't write a proper business letter. Business protocol? Fugadabout it!

Ashley is certainly not interested in paying her dues. Never has been, never will be. She is a concerned citizen and even has a plant in her cube. She believes her generation will change things. Doesn't that sound familiar?

### GENERATION Z (BORN AFTER 2000)

Meet Chloe. She's smart and can outchat anyone on Snapchat. Her parents are encouraging her to get her driver's license, although she can't understand why, since she has three ride-sharing apps available right at her fingertips. Chloe has had a device in her hand since she was a baby and may be more technology literate than those from any other generation.

The oldest cohort of Gen Z are just about out of high school, and some are currently holding down part-time jobs—on their own terms. They've learned quickly that companies need them more than they need companies. Things should really get interesting when the tables turn again and the labor market tightens, as this generation may have to work on someone else's terms.

Members of Generation Z will appreciate working in virtual teams more so than coworkers from other generations, as they are accustomed to working face-to-face with a screen in between. Many are used to operating five screens simultaneously (television, mobile, desktop, laptop, and tablet) and are easily distracted. As such, they prefer simple communication. Why waste words when one emoji will do?

# Seismic Shift: The Impact of the Changing Demographics on the Workplace

Managers today are struggling with how to keep everyone happy, given that we are experiencing record-low rates of unemployment and worker shortages in many parts of the world. As you can see from the descriptions of the generations in the workplace, there is no one-size-fits-all answer when it comes to keeping employees satisfied and

happy at work. However, there are practices that are appealing to all employees, regardless of age. Here are some options for you to consider.

1. **Be flexible**—Be willing to consider requests to modify work schedules, no matter how out-of-the-box these requests may seem. Sure, maybe no one in the organization has ever worked half the year in Boston and the other half in Miami, but does this mean it can't be done? Companies like CVS and Home Depot are offering their employees opportunities to fly the coop when the weather gets cold and to return to the nest as communities begin to bustle again. This allows them to retain experienced workers who are ready to hit the ground running when they return to work. Managers can also, by allowing this type of seasonal work schedule, adjust their staffing in locations to meet the needs of the surging population during peak times. Many smaller firms are now getting into the snowbird act, particularly with those workers who are on the road a lot. The cost to set up a home office these days is so reasonable that many employers are now more open to this type of option, particularly if saying no means losing a valuable worker. This approach allows older workers who are looking to retire an opportunity to continue work in a way that suits them.

   Let your workers solve their problems. If an employee comes to you and wants to do a job-share, then ask him to come back to you with the other person who is willing and able to take on the role.

   If an employee asks for time off to take care of an aging parent or an ill child, do whatever you can to provide her with the time she needs. When she returns to the workplace, she will be more committed than when she left.

   Speak to the owner of your company or to senior management to see if it's possible to offer phased retirement. Sometimes knowing you have the option to phase out of the organization at any time is more important that actually doing it. Phased retirement allows employees to reduce their work hours or responsibilities. Some employees will cut back their hours only to realize they prefer a full-time schedule. The option of phased retirement is attractive to individuals because they can continue to earn an income under more flexible terms while the employer gets to keep valuable employees that much longer.

2. **Succession planning**—Succession planning is a process whereby an organization ensures employees are recruited and developed to fill each key role within the company. This type of planning is

usually done by larger organizations, which have the resources to do this. But that doesn't mean you can't do this on your own. In fact, effective managers do this all the time, perhaps on a more informal basis.

Put together a chart of your current staff and their positions. Then take a close look at the skills required for each position. Now think about who you can move into each of these jobs, should someone leave. If you don't have anyone in your work group to fill a particular job, ask yourself what someone in your group would need in order to be ready to move into this role. Now begin to prepare this employee for the next step up by providing her with training, development, and coaching to ensure she is ready to move into this role when the time comes. Outstanding managers are always looking for ways to develop their people. They rarely worry about investing in employees who may leave them for another company because they know that if they treat them right, this person will be with them for a long time.

Some of you may be wondering why you would want to train your replacement. Here's why: Your boss may be hesitant to promote you if there is no one who can easily move into your job.

3. **Hire for potential**—If your organization is about to go through a period of rapid growth, or if your particular workforce consists of some fairly seasoned employees, you know it won't be long before you will need to pull from the younger ranks. It is imperative that you seek new hires who demonstrate they have the potential for growth. After all, these people may become your "A" team sooner than you think.

# Busting Common Myths Associated with the Generations

"They are not really interested in working." "They know nothing about technology." "They are just a bunch of crybabies." Enough already! I'm sick of people trying to shove *everyone* into nice little boxes so they can make the chart on their PowerPoint slides look nice. These are just some of the many common myths we hear about the generations in the workplace. This stereotyping has significantly hindered our ability to successfully unite the generations in the workplace. I'm proposing that we bust through these myths so you can focus on what you need to actively engage people throughout your workplace. The best way to

bust through these myths is to share some of the common ones. Below are four that you're likely to hear.

1. **Younger workers are lazy.** All you have to do is walk through the office after 5:00 P.M. and you'll see for yourself. Most of the younger staff are nowhere to be found. So of course we can assume they are lazy and they are not willing to put in the extra hours it takes to move up in the organization.

   I've interviewed hundreds of Millennials throughout organizations across the U.S. for work that I do regarding the generations, and the one line that keeps coming up consistently is "Don't mistake our ability to get work done quickly as laziness!" This group is not lazy. They are efficient. They don't believe they should sit in their cubicles doing busy work just because they work efficiently. I wish I had been as smart when I was their age. I wasted hours of my life shuffling paper, waiting for my boss to go home so I could depart!

2. **Older workers aren't interested in learning.** Really? Eighty-five-year-old Don Weedin, of Poulsbo, Washington, went back to receive his G.E.D. at age forty. Millions of older workers decide to move on from or leave their jobs every day because they feel like they are no longer learning.

   Many people, young and old, work because they like to be challenged. Just because you hit a birthday with a zero at the end of it doesn't mean your brain goes on holiday. Provide your mature workers with new opportunities to learn and see how they continue to blossom.

3. **Gen Xers have low levels of work commitment.** They'll leave you at a moment's notice. Really? Tell that to Gen Xer Michael Shipman, VP of Talent and Organizational Development for Hanover, Massachusetts–based Rockland Trust. He and many other Gen Xers in this organization are totally committed to the mission and goals of their company. Michael glows when he talks about Rockland Trust being recently named by the *Boston Globe* as "one of the 100 Best Companies in Massachusetts."

   A recent study conducted by Catalyst found that Gen Xers are very committed to their jobs and their careers. Fully 85 percent reported that their fate in their workplace mattered, and 83 percent said they were willing to put in far more effort than is normally expected to help their organizations succeed. People, regardless of age, will demonstrate high levels of commitment to their organizations if they feel they are making a difference.

4. **Older workers lack stamina.** Whatever you do, just make sure you don't tell your employee who runs the Boston Marathon every year that you believe she doesn't have the stamina to do the job. Mature workers are in better shape than those who have come before them.

   If you've been fortunate enough to catch Rolling Stones frontman Mick Jagger in concert, you know exactly what I mean. In an early interview, a young Jagger told a reporter that if he was still singing "Satisfaction" when he was in his forties, he'd kill himself. Today, in his early seventies, not only is he still singing "Satisfaction" in stadium shows, he's knocking it out of the park! Need I say more?

## Motivating Your Mature Workers

We discussed earlier what you can do to retain your mature workers. Now let's talk briefly about what you can specifically do to keep them motivated.

People like to be asked for their opinions, and this is especially true for mature workers. Consider setting up a mentor program, so mature workers can work side by side with younger workers to share their wisdom and expertise. While you are at it, establish a reverse mentoring program, where younger workers can share their knowledge with mature workers, who may benefit from hearing all those fresh ideas, not to mention all those tips on how to use and maximize technology!

Seek your employees' opinions, particularly if the company is trying to extend its marketing reach to a similar demographic. I often cringe when I see ads that are supposed to be targeted to my demographic. I wonder which twenty-something thought this particular message would resonate with people in my age group! When designing products for a particular segment of the population, ask those in your organization who fit the bill to provide input. This may prevent you from inventing a product or adding expensive features that will be deemed useless by your intended market.

Show through your actions, and not just through your words, that you are not planning on replacing them with a younger model anytime soon. (Of course, don't do this if your intent is quite the opposite!) This will help you create a workplace based on loyalty and trust, both necessary ingredients for engaging mature workers.

# Help! My Employee Is Treating Me Like Her Child!

I can personally relate to those of you who have had to put up with employees treating you as if you were their own child. Early in my career, I had a secretary who used to wag her finger at me when she was upset with something I did, just as an angry parent would wave her finger at a young child. It used to drive me crazy.

I finally couldn't take it anymore, so I decided it was time to have a talk with her. She was shocked to hear she was doing this. She was so accustomed to waving her finger at her own daughter (who was my age) that it had become part of her being. We both laughed when she apologized, and we came to an agreement that she would sit on her hands the next time she got upset with me!

The employee who is treating you like a child may have no idea he is coming across this way. Provide him with specific examples of what he is doing that makes you feel this way and ask for suggestions on what he believes can be done to improve this situation.

## Unleashing the Potential of Younger Workers

I'm a huge fan of the Millennials. Their capabilities are amazing! However, some people may never come to this realization because many Millennials enter the workplace like bulls in a china shop. I, on the other hand, see them more like stallions. With proper training and guidance, they can be groomed to become real competitors in the workplace.

Millennials want and need structure. If you toss a project on their desk while you are running by their cubicle, you'll have to deal with the consequences. By that, I mean that they may be in your office every ten minutes asking you for further clarification. Take the time to tell them exactly what you want done, and they will do it. Fail to do this, and it won't be long before you are off to the races, looking for a horse whisperer.

- To be successful in today's business environment, managers must be adept at leveraging generational workforce differences into opportunities. We begin by gaining an understanding of where people are coming from, so we can determine how best to support and manage them as individuals. We must familiarize ourselves with the differences and commonalities of each generation so we can tear down any barriers that are preventing our workforce from uniting.

- There is no one-size-fits-all strategy to keep workers satisfied and happy. However, there are best practices such as job flexibility and continued investment in the development of your people that are valued by employees of all generations.

- We will see dramatic changes in the landscape of the workplace as Baby Boomers begin to exit the workforce in droves. Some industries, like technology and retail, may be less affected by this shift, since these industries tend to employ a younger workforce. However, in many industries, including public utilities and educational institutions, the impact of the Boomers moving into retirement will be devastating. Examine your surroundings and plan accordingly.

- There are plenty of myths surrounding each of the generations. Do your best to ignore much of what you hear; instead, make your own observations and conclusions.

- Each generation has something to contribute to the workplace. Create mentoring and reverse-mentoring programs so that workers can shine while guiding others who may be less experienced in a particular area.

*I got promoted and had the responsibility of managing my best friend, who tried to, and did, take advantage of the fact we were best friends. Expected special treatment, didn't show up, and expected no consequences. My choices were to fire him or lose my job for being incompetent.*

*I fired him, for the right reasons, and walked away with a valuable lesson on managing departments that has held me in good stead throughout the years. In retrospect, he was toxic to the function of the organization I was trying to manage. Do what you know is right, and things will work out for the best, even if it doesn't seem so at the time.*

Ray McTier
*Management and Technology Strategist*
*Ray McTier Consultants*

# Dealing with Difficult Employees

## Strategies to Keep You Sane during Insane Times

Ask managers what they dislike most about their jobs, and the majority will say dealing with problem employees. Problem employees are a fact of life, so the sooner you learn how to deal with them, the easier your job will be. But wait, you may be thinking that if you do what I say and hire the right people, you're not going to have to worry about this.

Over time, people and circumstances change. Consider people you know who have gone through life-changing events. For example, can you think of someone whose personality shifted dramatically as they were caring for an aging parent or while they were going through a divorce? Or what about an employee who seemed to be the perfect worker until his salary was frozen?

It's best to be prepared for anything and everything. The worst that can happen is that you will never need these skills. But like a fire drill, it's best to know where all the emergency exits are located, just in case one day you need to use this information.

## Toxic Employees

Let's begin by defining a toxic employee. For our purposes, this is someone whose negative behavior and demeanor has an immediate effect on everyone he comes into contact with. Signs that indicate you have

a toxic employee in your workplace include infighting, backstabbing, passive-aggressive behavior (aggressive actions done in a passive or weak manner), antagonism, arguments or criticisms for the sake of being different, and an unwillingness to help out others in a culture that values collaboration. Toxic employees are highly contagious and often contaminate the rest of your workplace if you don't take immediate action. Usually, the only cure that works is removal.

Some toxic employees have no idea they are diseased. Often this is because no one has ever confronted them, for fear of their wrath. Think of these people as the bullies on the playground. Only this time, you're not five years old and your mom isn't there to make sure everyone plays nice.

The only way to take on a bully (or in our case a toxic employee) is to approach him head-on. Before you make your attack, you will need to be sure you are prepared for the battle. Begin by writing down all of the behaviors you have noticed and the impact these behaviors are having on the organization. You need to be very specific about the behavior you observe. For example, telling a toxic employee he has a bad attitude, which has been noticed by others, will do nothing but fuel the situation. The most likely response you will receive from him is, "What do you mean I have a bad attitude? I'm not the problem here. You are!" Right about now, you will probably want to run out of the room looking for a parent to take over.

Now imagine how the conversation might go if you provided this employee with specifics regarding your observations and the impact this employee's behavior is having on others. For example, you might say, "John, I noticed at our staff meetings that you do not let others finish what they are saying before you tell them why they are wrong. For example, last Friday when Bill was sharing his opinion on how to fix the software bugs that have been delaying the launch of our new product, you cut him off midsentence to tell him his ideas would never work. I don't believe you mean to do this. But when this does occur, I'm wondering if you've noticed, as I have, the reaction Bill and other members of the team have to your behavior. People seem to shut down and are no longer willing to work toward solving the problem."

In some situations, this will be a breakthrough moment. John may ask you to provide more examples, so be prepared to share more than one occurrence that you've noted. He may then ask you for suggestions on how he can change his approach. Be ready by having some answers to questions you can foresee.

What if things don't improve? You have a very short window to turn this behavior around. My advice is to come up with a performance

plan with your employee that includes exactly what you require and the specific dates by which you expect this employee to turn his situation around. Include exactly what will happen if this timetable is not met. For example, will the employee be put on a formal performance improvement plan or will he be terminated? Then be sure you follow up as you've stated so the employee knows you are committed to solving this problem, one way or another.

## My Employee Is Going through a Difficult Period: Avoiding the Shift from Manager to Therapist

We spend so much time at work that it shouldn't be surprising that the lines between work and family can become blurry. But even when it does happen, we are often unprepared. I recall early in my career having an employee come to me for what I thought was advice on a business-related matter. I spent two hours (which is way more than I should have) listening to him share his marital problems. Talk about feeling ill equipped! I was a twenty-four-year-old single woman who knew nothing about marriage, even less about divorce, and was still learning my new job. I wanted to be supportive, yet I felt way out of my depth. And I was!

An event like the one I just described may happen to you, so it's best to know what to do. A good place to start is by asking HR or your manager if your organization has an Employee Assistance Program (EAP). These programs are a great referral source for employees in need of professional services. All conversations are confidential, and services may have little or no fee.

What do you do if your organization does not provide access to an EAP? Look about for a nonprofit that might be able to assist your employee. Or suggest she speak with someone at her local church or synagogue who can guide her through this difficult time. It's best to locate resources *prior* to situations arising, so you have a place, other than the couch in your office, where employees can find help.

# Using Sugar to Sweeten an Employee's Disposition

There are times when good employees sour. When this occurs, think about when you first noticed a shift in this person's behavior. Was it right after you gave her an exceptional performance review and then had to tell her there would be no increase in her salary? Did it occur soon after the company announced layoffs? Or had you just been assigned another office to cover, which left you with less time to spend with this person? If you can identify where your employee may have gone off course, you may be able to redirect her so she comes back into the fold.

I'm asking you to think about these questions because if you can identify a specific event or events that have caused an engaged employee to become disenchanted, you may be able to make some simple changes to the way you've been working with her. Here's what I mean by this. If we take the example of the employee who received an exceptional performance review and no rise in compensation to go along with that, we can look at other ways of acknowledging this employee for her commitment. You could go to HR to see whether a promotion is possible. Or you could acknowledge this person's contribution to the team's success at your next staff meeting. You might grant this employee's request to telecommute a few days a week.

The one option you do not have available to you when an employee's attitude toward work becomes negative is to do nothing. The situation will not improve on its own and in most circumstances will only get worse. Acknowledge the problem, analyze your options, and then make a decision about how to proceed.

# Tools You Can Use to Reduce Conflict

When it comes to conflict, about the only thing we can all agree on is how uncomfortable conflict is for most people. People are reluctant to address problems they are having with an employee, a coworker, or even a boss. Yet pretending everything is fine certainly won't improve the situation. Here is just one example of why avoiding conflict with one of your direct reports isn't in the best interest of the employee, yourself, or your company.

I recently spoke with a client who was describing an employee who wasn't working out as he had hoped. His employee was refusing to

take on projects that were well within the scope of her job description. He also mentioned how unpleasant she was making life for everyone. Yet, instead of confronting this employee, he said he was going to wait for her to find another position within the company so he could be rid of her.

I suggested a different approach. Why not simply tell this employee that she has gone as far as she is going to go in his work group and that it is time for her to move on? This is certainly in her best interest as well as his, and more than likely will take less time than waiting for her to bid adieu on her own. He thought my idea was brilliant!

Now, I know that not everyone is willing or able to deal with conflict the way I do. But what if you could be more effective in asking for a change in behavior that might benefit both you and the person you are addressing? Would you then be willing to give it a go?

Let's begin by changing the way we view conflict. Whenever we think about conflict, we tend to give it a negative connotation. Yet conflict can be good. Here's why: Conflict fuels innovation. It helps take good ideas and make them great. Here is an example of what I mean by this. Have you ever noticed that the best ideas seem to come from other ideas? Think about what would happen if everyone went along with whatever was suggested and stopped there. Do you think innovative products like smartphones would exist if no one in the room challenged the idea that a phone could be used for more than just making and receiving calls? You can close your eyes and imagine the sparks flying in the room as each participant defended his or her position during that discussion!

Conflict can also be beneficial. Let's go back to my example of the manager who was choosing not to confront his employee. If he were willing to confront this employee and he did so in a way that allowed her to see why moving on was in her best interest, he would likely minimize the pain and disruption that is often associated with conflict. In this example, respectful confrontation might free an employee to find a position where she is valued as an employee, rather than being stuck in a dead-end job where her boss believes she is failing miserably. Her boss might even go as far as offering to help her transition out of the organization.

Conflict provides numerous opportunities for growth through improved understanding and insight. However, there is little chance of this occurring if both parties approach a situation prepared for the worst. Imagine how differently that interaction would be if you both approached the situation presuming the other person would like to resolve this issue amicably. You would then be working toward a shared

vision. An approach I learned from working with Libby Wagner, of Libby Wagner and Associates, offers two variations on what confrontation might look like in the workplace.

## SCENARIO NUMBER 1: THE OLD WAY

"That Tommy! He's always looking for the easy way out. But this time he's gone too far. The next time we meet, I'm going to tell him that I'm tired of receiving accounts receivable reports that do not contain the recommendations that I've asked for. I'm his boss. Not his babysitter!"

It's pretty clear from this scenario that things are really going to heat up in this meeting. Neither party will hear one another because each will be too busy placing blame. It's unlikely that much will change as a result of this interaction.

How do you think things might go if the boss entered the conversation with a new outlook? What would happen if the boss asked Tommy in a respectful way to change his behavior?

## SCENARIO NUMBER 2: A FRESH APPROACH

"Tommy, can we sit down and talk in private for a few minutes? I am confused. The last time we talked, you agreed to have the completed accounts receivable report on my desk by noon on Fridays, along with your recommendations for those accounts that should be moved into collections. Yet, in the last four weeks, you've only given me one report that included your recommendations. What is it that you need from me to better support you with this task? How can we move forward?"

The demeanor of the boss during this confrontation feels a lot different than it did in the first scenario. Here, we feel like the manager really wants to support his employee. He is respectful and is trying to be part of the solution. He hasn't let this situation brew for six months. Otherwise, he may easily have turned to scenario number one out of sheer frustration.

If you begin to view conflict as a way to improve your understanding of a particular situation, you will be less apt to be one of those people who has chest pains at the mere thought of dealing with a situation. In most cases, the other person is interested in clearing the air as well, so you can move forward together.

With practice, this type of conversation will feel less uncomfortable, and the experience will strengthen your leadership skills. You will also notice that for some reason, you seem to have fewer "problem employees" than you originally thought.

# Can This Marriage Be Saved?

I'm all for trying to salvage a relationship. But I also know there will be times when, regardless of what you do, you will not be able to save the relationship. So how can you tell if you should even bother? Here are some questions you must ask:

1. Is the other person interested in working on the relationship, or has she thrown in the towel? Remember, it takes two people to make a relationship work.
2. How much will I need to invest in this situation, and will it be worth the return? It may be less costly to cut the cord and begin anew.
3. What is the opportunity cost of spending my time on this? In other words, if you are spending hours every week with this employee, what might be slipping through the cracks?

# Signs This Relationship Cannot—or Should Not—Be Saved

There are clear indicators that some relationships cannot be repaired. If you fail to recognize these signs early on, others will question your judgment. Here are a few examples:

1. Your employee goes to your boss and tells her you are inept. It's very difficult to rebuild trust with an employee who has just stabbed you in the back.
2. An employee knowingly divulges confidential information to your competitors. This person has decided to play for the other team. Trade him before he does more damage.
3. Your work styles are incompatible. For example, you require work to be completed when it is assigned and the employee pays no attention to deadlines.

In time, you will learn that there will be situations that are not going to work out, no matter what you do. Relationships require two parties working together toward a common goal; the relationship won't survive if you aren't working in concert. You have a choice to make: Are you willing to let go of the other party so you don't go down

with him, or will you continue to hang on until you are the one who is asked to leave?

---

## KEY LEARNING POINTS

- Problem employees are a fact of life, so the sooner you learn how to deal with them, the easier your job will be. These problems aren't going to go away if you simply ignore them. You must take action before others in your work group start to show the same symptoms.

- It only takes one toxic employee to destroy everything you've built. The attention you should be giving to building on the strengths of your other employees is now being spent trying to minimize the damage being done by your problem employee. Don't wait for the toxicity to seep into the rest of your work group. Taking action may mean immediately extricating that employee from the workplace.

- Not all confrontation is bad. In fact, some confrontation is good. Confrontation fuels ideas that lead to innovation. Before you label someone as a difficult employee, be sure you aren't doing so simply because she isn't agreeing with everything you say.

- If you are planning to confront a toxic employee or an employee who appears to be more challenging to work with than others, approach the conversation fully prepared. This means coming into the meeting with specific examples of how her behavior is directly affecting the team and the objectives you are trying to achieve. Be prepared for push-back. Frame the conversation in a way that the employee can easily see why it would be in her best interest to immediately change her behavior.

- There will be times in your life as a manager where you will be asked to play the role of a therapist. Instead of trying to provide personal advice, suggest resources where employees can locate the help they need during difficult periods in their lives. Don't attempt to take this on. You do not want to be responsible for what may happen next.

- Sometimes, no matter what you do, you will not be able to save the relationship. Give it your best shot, but be ready to move on if the relationship is not worth saving. As you become more experienced, you will better be able to assess those situations that can be resolved and those that cannot.

---

*If you treat people well and you treat them fairly, it's pretty easy to gain respect. The ultimate recognition for me has been when people are willing to do something extra because they really trust me.*

*If you lead by example, walk the talk and make the right business decisions, you gain respect. This behavior also enables you to achieve a deep connection with your team that will allow you to move the organization emotionally to the next level—which is quite a unique place to be.*

*It's very easy to be successful, but not everybody understands how important it is to find the magic of human relationships. Having a special bond with your people will allow you to be more efficient and will help you achieve more than you thought was possible. Getting to the state where employees respect and love you is the ultimate destination for any leader.*

Marc Busain
*President*
*Heineken Americas*

# Should You Care if Your Employees Love You?

## How to Create a Respectful Workplace

As human beings, we have a natural tendency to want to be loved. But what happens when your desire to be loved interferes with your ability to lead? People who gravitate toward leadership roles tend to be charismatic. They work hard at keeping their audiences captivated and enjoy the adoration they receive from their followers. This is all fine and good, until their desire to be liked, or even loved, begins to cloud their judgment. In this chapter, I'll share some ways this can play out in the workplace, so you can avoid these pitfalls.

## College Buddies Rather than Subordinates

In their quest to be liked, leaders may drop their guard and become more informal with their employees than they should be. For example, a leader may join her staff at happy hour and reveal more than she should. There is nothing wrong with sharing a glass of wine with the team; however, things can quickly get out of hand when one glass leads to a bottle. Before you know it, managers are sharing drinking stories from their college days. Throw in a few shots of tequila, and all bets are off.

If you are to lead effectively, your followers must have a high regard for you. If you get sloppy during happy hour, they may look up to you all evening, but will they still respect you in the morning?

## Communicating versus Commiserating

The higher up you go in the organization, the lonelier it gets. You will find there will be fewer people you can confide in regarding your hopes and fears. It can happen to the best of leaders—eventually they stop communicating and start commiserating with other members of the management team and sometimes with staff.

In trying times, your team is looking for a strong leader, someone who they are confident will be able to guide their ship through choppy waters. The last thing they need to hear is a leader expressing doubt about the direction the captain is taking the crew. If you find that you need a sounding board, consider hiring an executive coach or joining an association where you will find like-minded people. Then be sure you return to the business of communicating to your team in a positive way, so when you turn around, you actually have people following you.

## Going with the Flow, Even though the Company May Be Racing toward a Waterfall

No one likes to be known as the person who bucks the system or, even worse, the person who tells the boss she is about to make a huge mistake. These kinds of people quickly become outcasts. To avoid this, many will go with the flow. They carry out the orders of top management, knowing these decisions will have a negative impact on the business.

One extreme example of workers following the dictates of top management with catastrophic results is the spaceshuttle *Challenger* disaster that occurred in 1986, when the spaceship broke apart seventy-three seconds into its flight, leading to the deaths of its seven crew members. The investigation that followed found that the direct cause of the explosion was the malfunction of an O-ring seal on the right solid-rocket booster. The investigation also indicated that engineers had expressed concerns, but when push came to shove, they relented.

John Schwartz and Matthew Wald, in a *New York Times* article about the disaster, explored the idea of a phenomenon called "groupthink." Irving L. Janis, a Yale psychologist and a pioneer in the study of social dynamics, defined groupthink as "a mode of thinking that people engage in when they are deeply involved in a cohesive ingroup, when the members' strivings for unanimity override their motivation to realistically appraise alternative courses of action." This results in a false consensus.

Think about the situations where you have personally held back your opinion because of your need to be liked. In retrospect, was this beneficial to the team? Or would it have been better for all involved if you simply stated your honest opinion?

In your career as a manager, you may be asked to dismiss an employee the boss just doesn't like. You'll have some choices to make. You can go with the flow and carry out the execution orders, or you can present the reasons why this action may not be in the best interest of the firm. You may be thinking, am I going to be shooting myself in the foot if I make a big deal out of this? Perhaps; but if you state your case in a way that makes sense, you may actually propel your career forward. Your boss will see that you have a spine, which is something your boss knows will come in handy the higher up in the organization you move.

## BFF (Best Friends Forever)

It's only natural that the people you work with eventually become long-term friends. After all, you spend most of your waking time working together. You may even socialize after work or on weekends. It's nice having people you can confide in who understand exactly what you are going through. But what happens when your relationship goes from peer to boss?

Every day across the world, BFFs (Best Friends Forever) become boss and subordinate. This doesn't mean you can no longer be friends with that person. However, it certainly means there will be changes in the dynamics of your relationship. In these situations, it is best to lay out some ground rules so neither one of you disappoints the other.

You will want to clarify your expectations, now that you are responsible for this person's performance and compensation. You will also need to discuss anything he may have told you in confidentiality, before you become his boss. For example, if your friend-turned-direct-

report told you he thought specific members of the management team were inept, you may want to reassure your BFF that you will not be sharing his opinion with those people, who are now your peers. However, if he's shared information with you that you now feel compelled to discuss with others, you need to let him know this is the case so he is not surprised should the matter come up for discussion.

Be realistic. The likelihood that you'll still be invited to have lunch with the gang is fairly slim. And if you are invited, you may no longer want to go. You may find that your friendship was strictly based on your kinship at work. Now that this has changed, you may no longer have much to say to one another. Prepare yourself for some uncomfortable moments, until you get your footing back. Understand that you've crossed over a bridge, and you are now in the land of management. This is a whole new terrain, and you'll likely find that you'll be navigating without a compass. You may head off in the wrong direction, but eventually you'll find your way back.

## Avoidance: Are You Doing Your Employee's Work Because You Don't Want a Confrontation?

How many times this week have you said to yourself, "I'll just do it myself"? Maybe you said this because you thought it would take less time to do something yourself than to provide directions to someone else. Or, more likely, you've said this because you've asked this person for something more times than you can count and it still hasn't been done.

Some conflict can be good. The key word here is "some." If you find yourself regularly avoiding these types of discussions or if conflict has become the norm, then it's time to do what you are being paid to do. If the effort required to turn this situation around (assuming it *can* be turned around) exceeds the value you will receive by doing so, consider replacing this employee with someone who will make it a point to do what you ask.

# With All Due Respect: Creating a Workplace Where People Feel Valued

Pull out a piece of paper and draw a line down the middle of it. On the left-hand side write the words "Low levels of respect," and on the right-hand side write the words "High levels of respect." Then describe how it feels when you are in a work environment where people deliver low and high levels of respect. Which side of the equation do you want to be on?

You may have noted on the left-hand side feelings like frustration, low levels of enthusiasm, little desire to excel, and so on. The right side of the paper likely features words and phrases such as feel valued, excited, enthusiastic, and willing to go the extra mile. It may seem obvious that you want to create a workplace where people are respected and feel valued. Yet all too often, this is an area where managers fail miserably.

Here are some ways you can build a workplace where people feel like they are always working on the right side of this equation.

**Listen more, talk less**—You may think you are already doing this, but chances are you are still doing most of the talking. Allow people to finish their sentences before jumping in. When an employee shares a challenging situation with you, don't assume he wants you to provide him with an answer. He may merely be processing his thoughts out loud. Ask him if he is seeking advice before providing it.

**Be genuine in your communication**—Have you ever worked for a boss who seems to tell all employees they are doing a great job, even though it's fairly obvious this is not the case? Don't be that guy! If you truly believe someone deserves your praises, then give it to her. If you really are worried about an employee who is going through a difficult time, then show empathy when you communicate with that employee. You can do this by reflecting back some of what was just shared.

**Collaborate**—Ask people for their opinions and listen to their ideas. Involve them when appropriate, and be sure to give credit where credit is due.

**Provide feedback**—People really want to know how they are doing. When giving feedback, be very specific so your employees know what behaviors they should repeat and what behaviors they should avoid repeating.

**Respect people's personal time**—You may be able to work nights and weekends because you have few family obligations, but that doesn't mean everyone is in your situation. Refrain from calling before-office-hours meetings and asking people to work late into the night or on weekends, unless the situation is so dire that it cannot be avoided.

**Deliver praise loudly and clearly**—If an employee has done an exceptional job taking care of a customer's needs, acknowledge that employee in front of her peers. Better yet, do it in front of the customer.

---
## KEY LEARNING POINTS
---

- It's human nature to want to be loved. Just make sure your desire to be loved doesn't interfere with your ability to lead.
- If your BFF is now your subordinate, then it's necessary to outline your new expectations clearly, given the change in your relationship; everyone must be clear about the rules of engagement.
- There is no place in management for commiserating with your team members. If you need someone to talk with, consider hiring a coach or joining an association with like-minded members.
- Avoiding confrontation is not an option for managers, particularly if the issue is related to performance.
- Creating a workplace where your employees feel valued and respected is a vital part of your job as a manager. You can control the conditions that turn this dream into a reality.

---

*As a regional manager for a technology services firm in 1988, I was abysmal at hiring and retaining people. My right-hand person (assistant) was a brilliant con artist who, for one year, was running her husband's contracting business from the office. She used our office supplies, phone system, and time on the job. I always wondered why she acted so scattered and disengaged. Instead of broaching the topic with her, I ignored it. One year later, she "suddenly" resigned. Lessons learned: Ignoring behaviors and only focusing on skills is very costly. Hiring for behavior is equally (if not more) important as skill. In retrospect, I wish I had attended some management training to learn this.*

Lisa Nirell
*Chief Energy Officer*
*EnergizeGrowth LLC*

# Performance Management

## Do I *Really* Have to Do This?

When it comes to performance management, more and more employees are rating their managers as needing improvement. That's no surprise, considering how distasteful both managers and their employees find the process. I have my theories as to why this is so. I believe it all starts at the top. The attitude toward managing performance and conducting effective performance reviews begins with the chief honcho and filters down through the organization. Consider the following scenario: The CEO believes that people at the executive level should be self-starters and therefore should be able to manage their own performance. Therefore, he pretty much lets his people manage their own performance. Every once in a while, he'll give a pat on the back when an executive does something worth noting. But that's about it when it comes to feedback. Come review time, it's not uncommon for an executive to simply see an increase in her paycheck without any formal conversation regarding her performance. Some of the better CEOs will at least take the executive to lunch and may spend fifteen or twenty minutes talking about performance-related issues. They will then quickly move onto topics related to future projects or sports, while finishing the meal off with a round of cappuccinos.

The executive or member of senior management has received the message loud and clear: Managing performance is not highly valued by the organization. Therefore, invest as little time and effort as possible. This type of behavior flows down through all levels of the organization. If you don't believe me, ask the millions of people who are still waiting to receive performance reviews that were due months ago.

Managing performance can be an overwhelming task if you try to take it on all at once. Those of us who have vowed to do some spring cleaning of our homes know what happens when we try to take on more than is humanly possible in a short span of time. Pretty soon, the leaves are falling and little has changed in the way of clutter. That's because the idea of tackling a monumental task is overwhelming to most people. But what if you could break this huge project into manageable chunks? Could you commit to cleaning out your desk this week and a bathroom cabinet next week? How would it feel to look back in six months and realize that you've been able to accomplish a goal that seemed insurmountable? The same process can be used to manage performance. Break this process into manageable moments so you can provide employees with meaningful feedback throughout the year and inspire excellent performance, all while keeping your desk clutter free!

## The Performance Management Cycle

The performance management cycle begins on day one and ends the day the employee leaves the firm. At times, you may find yourself more involved in this process than at other times. This will depend on how smoothly things are running in your organization as well as the needs of your particular employees.

## Establishing Expectations

Begin by setting aside time to get to know the people you will be managing. This will help you effectively assess the strengths, weaknesses, and personal career aspirations of your employees. This conversation will also help you gain insight into how best to provide feedback. For example, you may learn that a particular employee responds best when given immediate feedback, whereas another needs evidence that a problem exists before he is willing to make any changes in his behavior.

As an employee, it's difficult to know what is expected of you if no one ever tells you. I can speak from personal experience. I once had a manager tell me during my review, "You are not meeting my expectations, although I'm not sure I ever told you what they were." And to think, this woman had an MBA from Harvard. Maybe Mindreading

101 is taught at Harvard, but it certainly isn't a course offering that I have ever seen. As a manager, you need to provide your people with clear expectations and ongoing feedback. This way, employees know *exactly* what is expected of them and they will also know how they are faring all year long, rather than only at review time.

## Performance Development Cycle

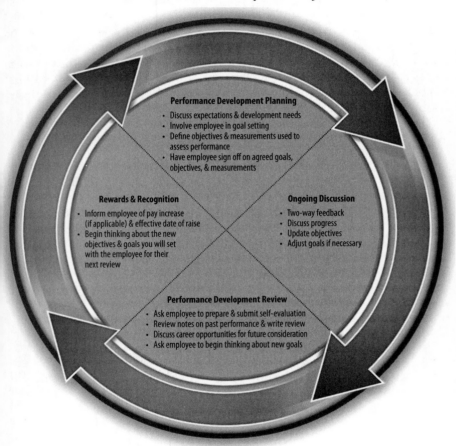

**Performance Development Planning**
- Discuss expectations & development needs
- Involve employee in goal setting
- Define objectives & measurements used to assess performance
- Have employee sign off on agreed goals, objectives, & measurements

**Ongoing Discussion**
- Two-way feedback
- Discuss progress
- Update objectives
- Adjust goals if necessary

**Performance Development Review**
- Ask employee to prepare & submit self-evaluation
- Review notes on past performance & write review
- Discuss career opportunities for future consideration
- Ask employee to begin thinking about new goals

**Rewards & Recognition**
- Inform employee of pay increase (if applicable) & effective date of raise
- Begin thinking about the new objectives & goals you will set with the employee for their next review

If you are in one of those environments I described earlier, where clear signals from the top indicate that little value is placed on the management of performance, then you have an opportunity to break the mold. Effective performance management is the cornerstone of

engagement, from goal setting to reward to recognition. As a new manager, you can directly impact employee engagement just by the way you choose to handle the performance management cycle.

In order to establish goals and expectations you need to be familiar with the specific duties and responsibilities associated with the position your employee is filling. This information is generally found in the job description. If you work in an informal office environment where there are no written job descriptions, you may ask your employees to list up to ten areas where they devote most of their working time. Check with your human resources department or ask your employees to provide you with copies of any goals that have been established prior to your arrival. Refrain from making any drastic changes if it's close to your performance review time, since they will have little time to achieve new goals before their reviews.

## Writing Goals and Objectives

Here are some handy guidelines for creating performance goals.

1.  **Involve the employee in the process**—There is nothing worse for an employee then being handed a set of goals and being told this is what is expected. This approach provides employees with little control over their own future. Some employees are conflict averse. They may agree to the goals, knowing the standard is impossible to achieve. Others will simply quit. Instead, begin with, "What do you think you can achieve?" Go from there and discuss your expectations.
2.  **Goals should be specific and measurable**—The employee should know exactly what he must do to achieve the agreed-upon goals and how each goal will be measured. This way, there will be no surprises come review time. When being specific, be sure you leave employees room to determine how best to achieve their goals.
3.  **Keep goals realistic**—I'm all for stretching people, but keep it real. By that, I mean that you should set goals that encourage growth, not destruction. For example, setting goals that require a salesperson to double her sales without additional support would not be advisable. This is a goal that feels impossible to achieve. Instead, specify a reasonable percentage of growth that you both agree is obtainable.

# Continuous Feedback

Believe it or not, employees want and need your feedback. Without it, they cannot improve. The philosophy of some managers is "if you don't hear from me, things are fine." But heaven help the employee the day he actually does hear from the manager! Wouldn't it be better, for all involved, if feedback was continuous? Then no one would be left guessing if he was performing at a level that was meeting or even exceeding the expectations of his boss. People could be making adjustments along the way, rather than waiting to do so until after they've received their annual performance review.

# The Performance Review

This is the part of the performance management cycle that many managers dread. Why? Because over the period under review, they have either failed to establish measurable goals or they have provided little, if any, feedback to the employee. This is of particular concern if the review is one that is not going to be glowing. Or, the manager doesn't fully buy into the evaluation forms that he is required to use. Regardless of your feelings toward this process, it's your job to provide employees with their annual or, in some cases, semiannual performance reviews. Therefore, you might as well master this skill.

# Overcoming Performance Management Anxiety

It's very common to feel anxious when you have to do a task that you dislike or when you don't feel fully prepared to do something. Performance reviews usually fall into both these categories for both new and experienced managers. But it doesn't have to be this way if you follow this time-tested advice:

**Collect documentation along the way**—It's difficult to remember what someone did last week, never mind last April. Now add ten or more employees to the mix and see how well you do! It's actually impossible for managers to remember all the details needed to put together an accurate performance review. That's why I recommend creating individual folders for each of your direct reports, which should be kept in a locked drawer. (Note: If you don't have a locked drawer,

keep the files at home.) Every time an employee does something worth noting, either good or bad, or whenever you have a conversation with an employee regarding her performance, write a brief note and slip it into the file. Remember to date the note, in case an employee asks you for specifics regarding a situation that you may be discussing again. Pull this folder out when review time rolls around and you'll be good to go. Your stress level has probably dropped two notches just knowing that you have everything you need to get started.

**Continuous feedback**—As we noted earlier, it's not uncommon for managers to reserve feedback for review time. This approach does little to foster open communication and transparency. When this occurs, employees often report feeling shocked and frustrated by what they are hearing.

Managers should schedule brief meetings throughout the evaluation period so employees know exactly where they stand at all times. During these meetings, managers may, with the input of their employees, decide to adjust the measurements that will be used to assess performance, particularly if major changes have taken place in the organization. Meeting more frequently also provides employees with ample time to make needed course corrections, which will boost productivity immediately.

**Honesty and transparency**—It's never easy to tell an employee he must improve. However, not telling him or being partially truthful isn't doing the employee any favors, nor will it help you establish yourself as a credible manager. Managers don't get the option of choosing to ignore performance-related issues.

You need to be fully prepared, especially when delivering a performance review that may be contentious. Write down specific examples of observed behavior that you will be sharing during your discussion with the employee. Refrain from including examples that may be perceived as hearsay. Reframe examples in a positive way. For example, if you plan on coaching Jim on his tardiness during his review, you may instead discuss the importance of being on time. Let him know why it is in his best interest to be more reliable (e.g., he may be invited to participate on a highly visible project; you will be able to recommend him for the telecommuting program, which he has expressed interest in, etc.).

An employee may come right out and ask you if you believe he will be able to move past this and be successful in the company. Here's

where transparency comes in. You can answer "yes" or "I don't know" if this is what you are really thinking. However, if it's clear to you this person is not going to succeed no matter what he does, then you must answer the question in a way that is honest but also doesn't wind up putting you in the middle of a lawsuit. You can simply say that you believe there are other opportunities out there that will be a better fit for this person. Then move the conversation toward how you might work together to help him transition.

**Managing nonperformers out of the organization prior to review time**—Why do so many managers think they have to wait until review time before they can begin the process of terminating the relationship with an employee? I'm often asked on the eighty-ninth day of a person's employment whether it's okay to terminate someone before she receives her ninety-day review. I usually ask the manager when they realized things weren't working with this employee. They usually say it was within the first thirty days. Yet, here we are almost two months later and we have an employee onboard who should have gotten off the train at the last stop.

Many companies have a ninety-day probationary period, which they may call an orientation period. This is done to remind the manager to check in with new employees frequently. This does not mean that you need to give people a full ninety days to become productive. That's like the equivalent of dating someone for an additional two months, even though it's clear after the first week that things are not going to get any better. That would be crazy, right? So why continue a work relationship that appears to have little potential of improving? Most likely, it's because we want to believe things will get better or we are secretly hoping the person will quit before we have to fire him. Take it from me, people are doing their personal best during the first ninety days. If you have done your job and have provided the employee with the training and feedback he needs and things haven't improved, the situation is not going to get better. If it truly is a matter of fit and you believe this person can be successful in another job within the organization, then help him transfer to another department. If you don't believe this is so, then transition him out as soon as it's apparent that no amount of coaching is going to improve the performance.

# Why Self-Evaluations Are Your Friend: Avoiding the Dreaded Look of Surprise When Conducting Reviews

What if you knew exactly what someone was thinking when it came to her performance? Would this information help you do a better job of preparing the employee's performance review? Luckily for you, the information is there for the taking. All you need to do is ask for it. Many companies include a self-evaluation form as part of the performance review process. This is where employees get to rate their performance. The completed form is then given to the manager before she writes the review. I suggest asking employees to provide you with a self-evaluation, even if that is not part of the formal process. This exercise will help you prevent the dreaded look of surprise when you are thinking one thing and your employee is thinking something else. If you've done your job well and you have had brief conversations along the way, then you shouldn't be caught off guard by anything stated in the self-evaluation.

But what if the self-evaluation doesn't resemble the performance of the person who resides in the cubicle outside your office? This does happen. This is a clear sign that there has been a disconnect. The employee believes one thing and you believe the opposite. You need to ask yourself the following questions before proceeding further:

- Was I specific enough when I communicated my expectations?
- Have my expectations changed, and I failed to communicate that to my employee?
- Am I evaluating the employee on the same job he was brought in to do, or did the job change midstream and I failed to adjust the goals?
- Have I provided the employee with ongoing feedback?
- Is there anything that I might have done to cause this disconnect?

If, after asking these questions, you realize that you have contributed in any way to this situation, then you need to figure out where your responsibility lies. If you haven't given an employee any feedback regarding an area where he is not meeting expectations, then perhaps you both agree to leave that goal on the list for the next review. This way, the employee isn't penalized for something that was not entirely

within his control. In the end, your job is to build on that person's strengths and to prepare him for success. You do this by keeping the lines of communication open, even when the unexpected happens.

---

## KEY LEARNING POINTS

- Managing performance is a process, not a one-time event. This means you should be conducting ongoing conversations related to goals, measurements, and career objectives throughout the management performance cycle.
- Performance management isn't something that you do *to* your employees. It is something that is done *with* your employees.
- The performance management cycle is a circular process that begins on day one and ends the day the employee leaves the firm. First, you must establish expectations so people know how their performance will be measured. You then involve employees in writing specific goals and objectives. From time to time you check in with employees to answer any questions they may have and to help them stay on track. The final step is providing each employee with a written performance review that captures the discussions you have had over the review period.
- Employees want and need continuous feedback. This means that you must provide positive reinforcement as well as guidance on what employees can do to improve their performance. When giving feedback, be specific. This way, the employee knows exactly what you'd like to see him do or not do in the future.
- The best way to overcome performance review anxiety is to enter into the conversation prepared. Collect documentation along the way, provide continuous feedback, and be honest and transparent in your communication.
- Performance self-evaluations are a manager's best friend. You have an opportunity to learn how an employee views her own performance before you write the performance review. An employee's self-evaluation could also provide you with additional information that you may have forgotten. You may also learn that there is a disconnect between what you are communicating and what the employee is hearing, if there is a huge discrepancy in what the employee has written and what you are thinking.

---

*You go through the full range of emotions as a manager terminating an employee.*

- *You are angry that you must do it.*
- *You are sad because you know this event will change the employee's life in the short term.*
- *You feel a little humiliation, because you may or may not have been in the same position and those same emotions rise up, no matter how many years ago it took place.*
- *You feel relieved because the termination is no longer keeping you up at night.*
- *You feel a sense of freedom because the "problem" has finally been resolved.*
- *Once it is determined that the employee will be terminated, you want to get it over as fast as possible.*
- *Even though many won't admit it, there is a sense of gratification knowing you gave the employee every chance to succeed.*

*When I do it again, I will shorten the process greatly.*

Patrick Hollister
*Former Regional Sales Manager*
*Fujitsu Components America, Inc.*

## CHAPTER TEN

# You're Fired!

## Timeless Tips for Tactful Terminations

O ne of the unpleasant realities of being a manager is that occasionally an employee does not work out or business needs dictate a reduction in payroll costs. Letting an employee go is never easy, and the way you do it can have a lasting impact on both the employee and the survivors—those employees who remain with the organization. Approaching the situation in a respectful manner will minimize the damage and disruption that is often associated with employee terminations.

Every manager should be required to view the movie *Up in the Air*, starring George Clooney. The film is an adaptation of a novel of the same name. In the movie, Clooney plays a professional corporate downsizer who travels around the country terminating unsuspecting employees on behalf of their bosses, who don't have the guts to do it themselves. Although the novel is fiction, similar occurrences happen daily all across the globe.

Case in point: A close friend of mine shared with me the story of her brother-in-law, who recently had someone he'd never met or spoken with appear in his office to tell him his services would no longer be needed. End of story—he got no explanation as to why he was being let go, nor was he given any opportunity to tie up loose ends or say his goodbyes. No one ever mentioned his performance was lacking or that the firm was experiencing financial difficulties. To this day, he doesn't know why he was let go, because his former employer refuses to return his phone calls. The man spent weeks on his couch in a state of anger and depression, which scared the daylights out of his family.

This particular story has a happier ending than many. This gentleman quickly received a job offer from a firm whose offer he had

originally turned down. However, he will carry this baggage around with him for the rest of his life. A day won't go by when he won't be peering out his office window, waiting for another stranger to show up to take his livelihood away.

I can't tell you for sure whether the man described above deserved to be fired. However, I can say for certain that he didn't deserve to go out this way. His anger and resentment weren't based on being let go because of economics. It was based purely on the way he was treated.

Organizations today are highly concerned about lawsuits from disgruntled employees who have been let go. I'm here to tell you, they should be. Managers are given marching orders to "get rid of" certain employees; inexperienced (and many experienced) managers don't have the guts to push back and say, "I don't believe this is the right thing to do, for the following reasons." So they do as they are told, with little thought as to what they can do to soften the blow.

Companies tend to treat employee terminations as if they were throwing a surprise party. Invitations are secretly sent to those who will be involved in the preparations. Private meetings are held before or after hours to ensure the "guest of honor" is not aware of the event that is about to take place. Every detail is nailed down prior to the big event, including what "gifts" (also known as termination packages) will be presented. Then everyone waits for the big day, usually a Friday, because we know the people attending will need the weekend to recover from the event.

This is wrong. Employee terminations should not be a surprise, unless a natural disaster has created the need to shut down a company immediately. If you are doing your job and managing performance, the employee should be fully aware things aren't going according to plan. If he does not know this, then perhaps you have failed to be specific enough in your conversations regarding your concerns, or maybe you haven't warned him that his job is on the line.

The way you handle the termination process will impact more than just yourself and the employee. Here's why: In the old days, companies only had to worry what former employees might say about them at a cocktail party. Today, that party is going on 24/7 on sites like Glassdoor.com, where people are encouraged to rate their current or former employers and include comments; on Facebook, where people have more friends than they can name; and on sites like Twitter, where bitter employees can do serious damage with only 140 characters. Coworkers, clients, and potential customers may be reading these

posts, which are of course one-sided. But that doesn't matter. In today's world, if it's on the Internet, it must be true!

## Gathering Your Ammunition: The Art of Documentation

It's time to stop thinking about yourself for a moment and instead think about your people. Conversations surrounding performance improvement are difficult, but they are necessary when people need to step up their performance. If you reframe the way you enter into these discussions it will become easier to have them. Consider the conversation as an opportunity to help someone get back on track. Remember, people can't improve if they have no idea they need to improve. But you must also keep in mind that, in the end, there still is a possibility that things may not work out. Therefore, you want to be sure you have documented all conversations related to performance. Otherwise, you may be told by your manager or someone in human resources that you have to retain this employee until there is enough written documentation to support your decision and to protect the company in the event of a lawsuit.

So what exactly should be documented? Write down the date and time of the discussion, as well as details of *any* conversations you have regarding performance improvement. Include the employee's reaction to the discussion as well as the time frame in which you agreed to address the issue again if the problem continues. Keep copious notes regarding observable behavior, such as frequent extended lunch breaks or excessive personal phone calls. All of this is referred to as documentation. You may even want to have the employee sign off on the agreed-upon action steps as a way of demonstrating conversations took place. This will also help increase the employee's level of commitment, as we know employees are more likely to follow through on something when they've agreed to do so in writing.

When pulled together, these notes paint a picture that may be viewed by others, should the situation escalate. Therefore, it is important to think carefully about how you present your documentation. For example, you may have a mature employee who appears to be struggling with meeting his sales objectives. You believe this is because he lacks the same level of stamina and enthusiasm as his coworkers. Here's what you *don't* want to say in your write-up: "Martin is unable to keep up with the younger salespeople on the team." That is, if you

don't want to be sitting across the table from Martin and his team of lawyers. This statement, as written, could be interpreted to mean that you believe Martin's inability to meet his sales objectives are related in some way to his age.

When writing documentation, stick to the indicators you've both agreed would be used to measure performance and you should be able to stay clear of any potential legal landmines. Here's an example of a better way to document a performance improvement conversation you might have had with Martin: "On July 15, 2016, I met with Martin to discuss the problems he has been having lately achieving his sales quota. For the past three months, Martin has missed his sales quotas by at least 20 percent. Martin assured me that he is committed to working harder toward his goals and will come back to me with a written plan, by the end of the week, outlining specifically what he is going to do to get his sales back on track. I have offered to join him on sales calls and provide him with whatever support he needs to succeed. Martin is aware that if he does not meet his quota in both August and September, further disciplinary action will occur, up to and including termination." With this approach, you will have a record of exactly what was said during your conversation with the employee and you will be able to refer to your notes to remind yourself what was agreed upon, before you take further action.

When documenting, be sure to date all your notes so you can establish a timeline of conversations that led to your decision to further counsel the employee or to end the relationship. Check with your boss to see if the company has a progressive disciplinary policy that requires a verbal, written, and personnel warning prior to releasing an employee for performance-related issues, as there may be specific forms you will need to complete as part of the documentation process.

# Pulling the Trigger: Knowing When It's Time to Execute

I know of so many managers who keep thinking things are going to get better. But they rarely do, especially if you have been forthright with your employees and they know their job is on the line. We mentioned earlier in the book how your job is to build on people's strengths. You can't do this if you are spending most of your days dealing with an employee who should have been gone a long time ago.

One of the common reasons I hear managers use for not firing an employee is that they are concerned about the welfare of the employee and her family. I'm all for compassion, but what happens when the rest of the team stops pulling its weight and the company starts going down the tubes? You have to look at the big picture. You need to throw the low-performing employee off the ship, before she takes the ship down. Plain and simple, you have to save everyone else. Quoting from the *The Godfather*, Donald Trump famously used these words in his reality TV show *The Apprentice*: "It's not personal, it's business." If you've done your job and the employee hasn't, then it's time to say sayonara.

## Avoiding the Heart: How to Terminate Someone While Leaving the Heart Intact

If I didn't know any better, I'd say that some managers actually enjoy firing employees. Otherwise, they wouldn't do some of the things they do. Here are some examples:

**Your job's safe. Buy that new house!**—This is one of my personal favorites, as it actually happened to a colleague of mine. She asked the owner of the company three times if he thought it was a smart move for her to purchase a home, given the economic climate. He managed to quell her fears. That was, until he laid her off two months later because he was struggling to make payroll. So here she was, a single woman with a big fat mortgage to pay and no job.

**Thank God it's Friday. Oh, by the way, you're fired.**—Great, now the fired employee's got the entire weekend to do nothing but think about what has just happened. He can't file for unemployment benefits, nor can he begin to start calling his contacts at their offices, because it's now the weekend.

**Great job! Here's your raise. Did I mention that tomorrow will be your last day?**—This would be funny if it weren't true. A person was given an "exceeds standards" performance rating, along with an increase in salary, only to be told the next day she was being laid off. Let's hope she didn't spend that raise before she got it.

**Your job is to lay off the guy with six kids. I will then do my job and lay you off.**—This happened to me the first time I ever had to lay someone off from his job. I still recall how ill I was the night before,

just thinking about what I was about to do. I conducted the termination and waited in the conference room for my boss to come in and debrief with me. She did a little more than debrief me. She laid me off.

There is absolutely no reason any of these terminations had to go down the way they did. In the first scenario, the owner knew darn well his company was in trouble. He should have told his employee it would be prudent to wait, rather than encouraging her to enter into a commitment that could have ended in bankruptcy. Employers terminate people on Fridays to ensure the employee gets everything tied up before he is let go. Have a heart. Consider what is in the best interest of your employee before firming up the day. The only reason I can think of for an employer giving someone a raise the day before they are going to lay that person off is to help her receive an offer for a higher salary in her next job. And, of course, there is my own personal scenario, where it is evident that my boss didn't have the guts to do the dirty work herself, so she assigned it to me. That was one going-away present I wish she would have kept for herself.

So how can you do things differently and how will you know when you've left the heart intact? You'll know you've done a good job of conducting an employee termination when the conversation ends and the employee says, "Thank you." Yes, that's right. I've learned this from experience and I have the "thank yous" to prove it.

In the television show *The Apprentice*, Donald Trump made firing look easy. It may be reality television but there is nothing real about his terminations, as some of these people went on to achieve fame and fortune. In most cases, all your employees will receive is an unemployment check. So for those of us who live in the real world, here are timeless tips to help you smoothly transition employees out of the boardroom, or wherever they may reside in your organization:

1. **R-E-S-P-E-C-T**
   Living legend Aretha Franklin made this word famous when she sang about it in the summer of 1967, and it still rings true. Being terminated can be as stressful as a death in the family or a divorce. Recognize that this will be an extremely difficult moment for the employee and do your best to be respectful.

2. **Avoid surprises**
   As we mentioned earlier, an employee's termination should not come as a surprise to the employee. If you believe this will be the case, retrace your steps. A more direct conversation may be your next step, before you move to terminate the person.

When communicating your final warning to the employee, be direct. Let the employee know that if she is unable to turn her performance around within a specified amount of time, her employment will be terminated. Resist the temptation to sugar-coat your message or you will leave a bad taste in the employee's mouth come termination time.

3. **Be prepared**
It's easy to get pulled off course when terminating an employee. Plan what you are going to say and do your best to stick with your script. You don't know where this situation will wind up and you certainly don't want to explain to your company's labor attorney how you told this employee he was one of your stronger players, while simultaneously firing him. This move might have increased Donald Trump's ratings on *The Apprentice*, but it certainly won't do much to boost your career.

4. **Focus on performance**
So often, we can't place a finger on what exactly is going wrong with a troubled employee, so we credit what we have observed to a poor attitude. But experienced managers know they could find themselves on Court TV if they fire based on attitude rather than performance.

Focus your discussion on performance-related issues. For example, rather than telling an employee that you are firing her because she has a poor attitude, cite specific examples of how her actions have negatively impacted her ability to achieve agreed-upon goals.

5. **Document, document, document**
We've already discussed why it's important to document performance-related conversations when managing performance. It's equally important to write up the details of the final conversation while it is still fresh in your mind.

As a manager, you are responsible for protecting the company. Good documentation could be the difference between winning a lawsuit and giving away last year's profits, including your potential bonus, to the disgruntled terminated employee.

6. **The facts, ma'am, just the facts**
A common mistake made by managers who are conducting terminations is to go back through the entire work history to explain why someone is being let go. This is extremely painful and unnecessary. Your goal is to have the employee leave the conversation in one piece, right? Tearing the person apart, limb by limb, does

nothing but destroy the ego. Besides, at this point, there is nothing the employee can do to change the situation.

Keep the conversation brief. Let the employee know why he is being let go, when his last day will be, and any other information he may need as he leaves the firm. This may include information about unemployment benefits (information you may be required to provide, depending on the state where your company is located); health insurance information, if applicable; and details about any other services, such as outplacement, that he may be entitled to.

Allow the employee time to process what you have said. If he keeps asking for feedback, politely tell him that you are not going to go through the entire file again, as you've had these discussions. Then steer the conversation back on course so you can complete the process.

7. **It's not about winning**

In *The Apprentice*, it was all about winning, but unless your organization is part of a reality TV show, this should not be your ultimate goal. Your objective is to transition the employee out of the organization with as little fanfare as possible. This can be accomplished when you shift the power back to the employee. You do this by giving the employee a choice. You might be champing at the bit to say, "You're fired!" but it's a heck of a lot easier to have an employee say, "I quit," not to mention much cleaner from a legal perspective.

If possible, offer the employee an opportunity to resign. This allows the person to retain her dignity. She leaves the organization on what many will believe are her own terms, while you happily return to your office. If you remember that this is about respect—not winning—you will have employees thanking you on the way out. Just like on *The Apprentice*!

# When There Is More than One Victim: Handling Layoffs

You would think that by now companies would be really good at conducting layoffs, given all the staff reductions we've seen over the years. Unfortunately, most have not improved. Following are a few examples of the practices I've seen.

According to a report in the local paper, employees at a manufacturing plant were told to report to a mandatory meeting. At the meeting, they all received envelopes and were instructed to open them at home. Some opened them in the parking lot and discovered they had been laid off, while others found out they were spared. All of these employees were originally told their jobs were safe and that their hours would just be cut back.

In a similar move at another company, employees were called into a conference room and given assigned seats. They were told that when the boss gives the signal, they were to remove the sealed envelopes under their chairs and open them. You guessed it. These envelopes contained people's layoff notices.

Treating layoffs as if they were a game is unconscionable, and I hope you will never be asked to participate in such a charade. I bring these situations to your attention to point out that, as today's leaders, you can do things differently. Here's how:

**Eliminate the words "there will be no layoffs" from your vocabulary**—You can't possibly know this unless you have a crystal ball. Case in point: No one could have predicted the events that took place on 9/11, which had both an emotional and an economic impact on people across the globe. Revenues in the travel industry immediately spiraled downward as people stopped flying. The ripple effect was soon felt by businesses that served or were affiliated with the travel industry. Companies that never thought they would have to let people go had no choice but to either lay people off or close shop.

**Leave the cow herding to the cowboys**—It may be easier for you to herd people into a conference room and release them in one swoop, but is this what's best for those who have dedicated their working lives to you and the organization? Your people deserve better than that. Here's where the golden rule of treating people as you would like to be treated comes into play.

If you are required to lay off more than one person, set aside time to meet individually with each employee in a private office. Give employees ample time to ask questions and to compose themselves before escorting them from the room.

**Ease the transition**—Job hunting has changed dramatically over the past several years. Networking is no longer about who you know. It's now all about who you're connected with on social networks. If you are letting an employee go purely for economic reasons, then do what

you can to ease the transition. Agree to serve as a reference, if your company does not have a policy against providing references. Tell the employee you will gladly accept an invitation on LinkedIn to connect and suggest the employee let you know if there are any specific connections he would like you to contact on his behalf.

## Taking Care of the Survivors

During these tumultuous times, it's easy to forget about the survivors. These are the people who are "lucky" to still be employed. If you think people are going to put their heads down and continue to work really hard when those around them are being laid off, think again. This is an extremely stressful time for everyone, including those who are still employed. Each survivor is wondering what will happen next. Will there be more layoffs? Is her job in jeopardy? How did the company treat her peers who were just let go? (Employees want to know this, in case they are let go.) Who is going to do all this extra work? You need to be prepared to answer these questions.

As we discussed earlier, do not promise people there will be no more layoffs. However, you can say that to the best of your knowledge there are no plans (that is, if there *are* none) for future reductions. Find out what, if anything, the company has done to help those who have been let go. This way, you'll be able to tell those who ask, that people were offered a separation package and provide an overview of what the package likely entailed (for example, severance, extension of their health benefits, or outplacement services).

Any time an employee is let go, it's best to assemble team members immediately before rumors start flying. You *are* going to be asked why someone was let go, so you need to be prepared to answer this question. If it's a matter of economics, then it's fine to tell people cuts had to be made in order to ensure the company would weather the economic storm. But what if the termination was due to performance-related issues or, even worse, illegal conduct such as employee embezzlement or sexual harassment?

Here is how I suggest you respond if poor performance or wrongdoing is the reason for termination: "I'm not at liberty to discuss the details with you, but I wanted you to know that as of this afternoon Diane Smith is no longer with the company. I am not going to provide you with any specifics, out of respect for Diane and her right to privacy. If you have specific questions as to how this change will impact your

work, then set up a time to see me this week so we can discuss this. So, let's talk about how we will move forward so that nothing falls through the cracks."

Terminating people will get easier with practice. But the truth is, the day it becomes too easy is the day you should look for a new career.

---

## KEY LEARNING POINTS

- Letting an employee go is never easy, and the way you do it can have a lasting impact on both the employee and the survivors (those employees who remain with the organization). Approaching the situation in a respectful manner will minimize the damage and disruption that is often associated with employee terminations.

- The first time an employee hears there are issues with her performance should not be when you are terminating her employment. As a manager, you should be continuously coaching employees, particularly those who may be struggling with their performance.

- Document all conversations and observations regarding an employee's performance so you are able to proceed directly to termination, should the situation warrant. Failure to do this may result in you having to delay action, which could be detrimental to your career.

- When writing employee documentation, write up the details while the information is fresh in your mind. Include dates, times, and specifics regarding observed and measurable behavior. If appropriate, ask the employee to sign off on what has been written to increase his level of commitment.

- Layoffs do happen. While it's never easy to terminate people who have been doing a good job, sometimes it is necessary. Regardless of how many people you must release from your department, treat each person as an individual. Do your best to help them smoothly transition to their next opportunity.

- Take care of the survivors. These are the people you will need to pick up the slack. Keep them informed so they don't wind up relying on the rumor mill to provide them with information, which may be inaccurate.

- There are ways to conduct employee terminations that leave the employee's heart intact. You do this by being respectful, avoiding surprises, being fully prepared for the conversation, and, whenever possible, allowing the employee to exit on her own terms.

---

*You know you are ready for your next promotion when you no longer feel challenged by your current role and you're starting to take responsibility for areas outside your normal scope. When this occurs, you start thinking bigger than the role you are in.*

*You have to go in and ask for what you believe you can do. When doing so, it's got to be your best sales pitch. Be prepared to demonstrate capabilities and show what value you can add to the business. An "I can do this and take this on" attitude will serve you well.*

*If there is a person in the room shouting a bit louder, don't step back thinking maybe they can do it better. This is the time to believe in you. It can be quite beneficial to work with a coach to help you power through and obtain the promotion you've been working toward.*

Judith Hogan
*Corporate Practice Leader*
*Plantronics Europe & Africa*

## CHAPTER ELEVEN

# Becoming a Leader Others Want to Follow

Anyone can become a leader. The real differentiator is becoming the kind of leader others *want* to follow, which is what we've been working on throughout this book. If you've been applying the principles you've gleaned from this book, then sooner or later (hopefully sooner) you'll be ready for your next step—a promotion to the next level of leadership.

## Securing Your Next Role

I find that people wait much longer than necessary to go after the next promotion. This is especially true of women. In a 2012 McKinsey study titled "Unlocking the Full Potential of Women at Work,"[1] it was found that women seem to get stuck in middle management. According to McKinsey, a global consulting management firm, "nearly 140,000 women have already made it to midlevel management at these companies—about one-third of the women professionals in these organizations. But only about 7,000 have become vice presidents, senior vice presidents, or members of the C-suite."

---

[1] "Unlocking the Full Potential of Women at Work," McKinsey, 2012, www.mckinsey.com/business-functions/organization/our-insights/unlocking-the-full-potential-of-women-at-work.

McKinsey found that men are promoted on potential and women are promoted on performance. Even among the most successful women interviewed, more than half felt they had held themselves back from accelerated growth. Most said they should have developed relationships with sponsors earlier, because a sponsor would have pushed them to take opportunities—too often, these women said, they did not raise their hands or even consider stretch roles. They soon learned the importance of letting senior management know about their goals. One woman said, "The minute I became directive about what I wanted, my career went on the fast track."

The advice I'm about to give is not gender specific; *if you think you deserve a promotion, then ask for it!* Make a note of this. Put a copy on your bulletin board as a reminder of the importance of asking for what you deserve.

## Signs You Are Ready for Your Next Promotion

People often ask me how to know if they are ready for their next promotion. My response is, "You'll know." It's probably not all that helpful, but it's true. Here are three signs you are ready for your next promotion:

1. **You no longer feel challenged.** You used to come to work every day excited to see what the day would bring. Now you know exactly what to expect, and each day feels the same. For some people this might happen six months into the job and for others it could be six years. That's why I say you'll know when it's time to take on the next challenge.

2. **An opportunity falls into your lap.** I never planned to take my boss's job at age twenty-four. Yet I saw an opportunity unfold before me (she was fired) and I took it! Was I ready? Heck no, although at the time I thought I might be. But that didn't stop me from asking for her job. In hindsight, I may never have been ready, or if I was, the job might not have been available. If a door opens—run in! I promise you'll figure it out once you settle in. And remember, you can always hire a coach to help you accelerate your growth.

3. **You're having a hard time getting out of bed.** You used to look forward to Mondays and getting to the office. Now you start fretting on Sunday afternoon, because you dread going into work.

Your people deserve better and so do you. Figure out if you're simply bored with your job and ready for the next challenge or if you are no longer in the right organization. Then take the first step to make that change.

# How to Ask for a Promotion

Our eighteen-year-old son is currently going through the college application process. As expected, some schools are more difficult to get into than others. One in particular is a stretch, requiring a ton of additional work for what is a long shot. We're supportive parents, but we are also realists. Early on in the process, we laid it all out for our son regarding the effort he would need to put in to attempt to get into this school and the likelihood of acceptance. We tried not to be too discouraging, but I have to admit, I may have gone a bit too far. One day, our son stopped me in midsentence and said, "Mom, if I don't apply, I'll never know." My goodness. How could I argue with that?

I hope you'll take this lesson to heart. If you want something bad enough, you owe it to yourself to go for it. Ask for what you believe you deserve. If you don't, you may be passed over, or worse—the promotion will go to your colleague who made it clear to your boss he wanted the job. If you are okay with that, fine. If you're not, then do as I suggest.

## PRESENTING YOUR CASE

Just like my son, you have to prove you are worthy of consideration. Prepare your case and state a clear and concise reason why you should be considered for the job.

Focus on outcomes you've achieved while in your current position, instead of tasks. When possible, monetize those outcomes. For example, when you remind your boss about a new service you introduced to clients, be sure to include the dollar amount of the new revenue that's hitting the bottom line as a result of your initiative.

If you've been working on strengthening relationships with those above you, now is the time to ask for their help, especially if they'll have input regarding who will be awarded this position. Reach out and seek their advice. And don't forget to ask if they might be willing to put in a good word for you.

# What to Do if the Promotion Doesn't Go to You—This Time

The higher up you go in the organization, the stiffer the competition will be for promotions. There will be times when the promotion goes to you and times when it doesn't. Being passed over for a promotion is a turning point for many. Here's what to do if the promotion doesn't go to you—this time.

**Ask for feedback.** Ask your boss what, if anything, you could have done differently to have earned the promotion. Listen carefully to the feedback and work diligently to improve, so the next time a promotion opportunity comes up, you'll be the obvious choice.

**Decide whether you'll stay or leave.** You're at a crossroad here and have a decision to make. It could be a while before another promotion opportunity comes your way. Will you remain in place and put your full support behind your new boss? Or will you seek a higher-ranking position elsewhere?

**Seek another position in the organization.** You've got more options if you work for a larger employer than if you are employed by a small firm. If this is the case, exercise those options. Now's a great time to ask your boss for his support. If he likes you a lot, he's probably feeling bad that he wasn't able to award the promotion to you. See if he'd be willing to recommend you for a promotion elsewhere in the company or in another division.

Here's what you *don't* get to do. I've seen managers who were passed over for promotion working diligently to undermine their new boss. They think that by doing so, they'll prove it was a mistake to award the promotion to someone other than themselves. Don't be this employee. This behavior can lead to the beginning of the end of your career with your employer. Your job is to be an asset—not a liability.

## Five Steps You Can Take While Still in Place

For a moment, let's assume you've made the decision to remain in your current position either because you were passed over for promotion or you didn't feel ready for a promotion. Use this time to grow in place. Here's where to begin.

## PRACTICE THE THINGS THAT MAKE YOU UNCOMFORTABLE

Suppose you're averse to conflict. You'll do anything to avoid telling someone her work is not up to standards. Having read this book, you know how important feedback is to employees. For a moment, imagine the shoe was on the other foot. Wouldn't you want to know if your skills were lacking and what you can do to improve? The next time you encounter a team member who didn't get things done quite the way you hoped, pull her aside and provide feedback. Keep doing this until it feels natural to coach people, so they can excel.

## FOLLOW LEADERS YOU ADMIRE

Here's an exercise I'd like you to do. Jot down the names of at least three leaders you admire, along with the reasons why you chose these people. Now I want you to cross their names off and replace them with yours. Next, circle those traits you don't have—yet. Now you can clearly see what areas you need to focus on. Keep this list handy and review it weekly, until such time as you've mastered the traits that will ensure you make it onto someone else's list.

## WORK ON BECOMING A THOUGHT LEADER

You don't need a title to be a thought leader—the go-to person for someone in your field. What you need are thoughts, which I'm sure you have! Thanks to social media, it's easier than ever to achieve thought-leadership status. Here are some ways to get started.

- Write articles for your local trade association newsletter.
- Consider establishing a personal blog, and fill it with content around your area of expertise.
- Add articles to your LinkedIn profile.
- Volunteer to speak at your local Rotary Club or at a trade association chapter meeting.
- Subscribe to HARO (Help a Reporter Out),[2] a free online service set up for journalists to connect with sources, and respond when you see a query that is right up your alley.

---

[2] HARO (Help a Reporter Out). https://www.helpareporter.com/

- Use social media to promote speaking engagements, articles that have recently been published, and quotes in the media.

The idea here is to build a following and to be known as *the* expert in your field. This will help solidify your candidacy for the next level of leadership either within your organization or with another firm.

## CONNECT WITH OTHER LEADERS

The company you keep *does* matter. Who is usually the first to know about an opening that will be coming available on the management team? It's usually the people on the team. That helps to explain why many open positions are never posted. An esteemed member of the team recommends a candidate and everyone agrees. This may not seem fair, unless you're the person who has been recommended. In any case, it happens often, and it won't happen to you without the right connections.

It's easy to find a common connection with a leader who is above you. One way to do this is to check out the leader's LinkedIn profile. See what groups you have in common. Did you happen to attend the same university? Is this leader on the board of a nonprofit you are interested in volunteering for? Use this information to break the ice and start a conversation, which is the first step in relationship building.

## ADD VALUE DAILY

The best way to get noticed is to add value daily. Many people show up for work, do their job, and do little more. Then there are the rare people who find a way to add value every day. Those people become indispensable. You want to fall into the indispensable category. Here's why.

Suppose the next promotion comes down to you and another person. Your boss is going to think twice before giving the promotion to someone else. He'll rightfully be concerned you'll leave if that occurs, and that when you do go, there will be a huge gap to fill.

There are a number of ways you can add value. Here are a few.

- **Be one step ahead of your boss.** Let's say your manager asks you to survey customers regarding their satisfaction with a new service the company has rolled out. She gives you three questions to ask. You follow her direction, and while speaking with customers you realize that an additional question would provide valuable insight. You slip the question into the conversation. No

doubt your boss will be thrilled that you've given her key insights and that you've taken it upon yourself to improve the results of the survey.

- **Be *the* person who volunteers whenever your manager asks for additional help.** Have you ever noticed that whenever the boss asks for additional help, most people do whatever they can to avoid eye contact, for fear they'll be assigned more work? Make it a point to be the person who immediately raises your hand and volunteers to make your boss's life easier. No doubt your boss will take notice and will view you in a more favorable light than your coworkers.

- **Be part of the bottom line.** Not all tasks are equal. Seek out opportunities to work on projects that impact the bottom line. For example, suppose your boss needs help doing a cost-benefit analysis on the purchase of new office equipment, as well as a market analysis for a new product launch. Grab the new product launch project before your coworkers have a chance to raise their hands. Here's why this is not only a smart move to make, but the only move to make if you are at all interested in moving up. The product launch project will give you an opportunity to work directly with key executives from the sales and marketing team, who may be asked for their input the next time a promotion is being discussed by the executive team. These leaders will be counting on you for a very important project that will help to grow company revenue. Now compare this to the new office equipment project, which is an expense that could be cut at a moment's notice.

- **Be a problem solver.** In most companies there are a handful of people who are highly relied upon to solve problems. Become that person. Work on developing your problem-solving skills until they appear effortless to others. When problems arise, alleviate your boss's concerns by reminding her that you've got this. Then go solve the problem.

# Seven Practices that Distinguish Great Managers from the Rest

I've worked with lots of companies and can tell you this. There are a ton of mediocre managers out there at *all* levels of the organization.

That's why it's easy to set yourself apart from everyone else. I've identified seven practices that distinguish great managers from the rest. If you can master four or more of these, you'll be in pretty good shape!

## I. A LIFETIME OF LEARNING

Great leaders are always in learning mode. They subscribe to publications like the *Wall Street Journal* and the *New York Times* to stay abreast of current events and new trends. They read all types of books, not just business books, and they can readily converse on many topics. They engage coaches throughout their careers to help bolster their skills. They return to school to further their education and attend conferences to learn other points of view.

I know this list can feel overwhelming. I suggest you pick one or two ways to increase your learning and add more as your needs change and as time permits.

## II. PUSHING THE OUTER LIMITS

The people who usually get ahead are those who are willing to push the outer limits. They don't necessarily accept the status quo. Yes, in some organizations this can be risky. You'll have to weigh out the risk versus the reward and decide for yourself how far you're willing to push in order to move your ideas forward.

## III. REMAINING CALM AND CARRYING ON

The higher up you go in the organization, the crazier it seems to get. Experienced leaders understand that there will be highs and lows. They remain calm by trying to foresee situations that may put undue stress on their work group. They get in front of problems rather than waiting for problems to occur. They also surround themselves with a strong team to help them soldier through whatever may come their way. And some—okay, many—have a strong administrative assistant to ward off distraction and to keep them organized.

Take measures to care for yourself first, so you can help others. This includes scheduling vacation time well in advance and leaving work on time so you can make it to your wellness class.

## IV. PUTTING PEOPLE BEFORE PERSONAL GAIN AND PROFITS

I recently spoke to an executive who went way beyond the call of duty for one of his people (or shall I say former people). He told me the story of how he had to let an employee go because of a reorganization. This employee happened to have a child who was ill. He told her he would cover her health insurance until such time as she had a new job so her child would not be without care. He didn't have to extend himself for this employee. He did so because he puts people before profits. It's no wonder he has a team of people who are willing to do anything for him.

There will be times in your career when the call for profits or personal gain may cloud your vision. I hope if you're ever in the situation where you have to choose between the two, you'll choose people.

## V. INSPIRATIONAL LEADERSHIP

Leadership may not have a one-size-fits-all definition, but most acts of leadership do share a common goal: Inspiring change. Pope Francis' willingness to challenge tradition and bring people back into the fold is a noble example of inspirational leadership. He's leading a thorough transformation of the Catholic Church—rivaling any brand revitalization or corporate turnaround you could name. He leads with his heart.

Sir Richard Branson is another example of an inspirational leader who is pushing the outer limits of what we believe is possible. Rather than using his power solely for his own gain, he's using it to advance science. Although his company Virgin Galactic may have had some major setbacks, he is still persevering and inspiring others, like Elon Musk, to follow his lead.

You don't have to be the pope or a billionaire to be an inspirational leader. However, it certainly helps to be passionate about what you believe in and charismatic enough to get others to join in your vision.

## VI. THE POWER OF PERSEVERANCE

Hands down, the best leaders are those who persevere. Success on any level requires the ability to follow through, to execute a plan, and to stick with it.

In fact, sticking with it may be the very best predictor of success. In a series of studies by the University of Pennsylvania, researchers found that those who persevere are more likely to achieve success than those

who cannot or refuse to do so. Martin E. P. Seligman, Ph.D., commonly referred to as the founder of Positive Psychology, states, "Unless you're a genius, I don't think you can ever out-achieve your competitors without a quality like perseverance."[3]

A good plan might get you into the game, but sticking with it propels you into the winner's circle. Listen to any story about leaders you admire and no doubt it will include times in their life when they had to overcome setbacks.

When things get tough, listen to your self-talk and work toward turning the negative conversation in your head into a positive conversation. Rather than thinking, "Man, this is too hard. I should just quit," tell yourself, "I know this can be done. I just have to power through." A positive mind-set really does make a difference.

## VII. VALIANT VISION

Imagine working for a leader whose vision is ordinary. Lots of you don't have to imagine this, as this is currently your truth. Now think about what it might be like to work for a leader whose goal is to turn your industry upside down! This kind of determination is rare. Now imagine all the possibilities and how thrilling it would be to be part of something big.

Entrepreneur and billionaire Mark Zuckerberg could certainly rest on his laurels, yet he and his wife, Dr. Priscilla Chan, have chosen to push the envelope further. Zuckerberg and his team are constantly looking at ways Facebook can be used to improve lives around the globe. An example of this is the recent introduction of Safety Check. According to Zuckerberg's Facebook page announcement, "Safety Check is our way of helping our community during natural disasters and gives you an easy and simple way to say you're safe and check on all your friends and family in one place."[4]

On a personal level, Chan and Zuckerberg pledged $3 billion over the course of the next decade to work on curing, preventing, and

---

[3] "Grit: Perseverance and Passion for Long Term Goals," Angela L. Duckworth, Department of Psychology, University of Pennsylvania; Christopher Peterson, Department of Psychology, University of Michigan; Michael D. Matthews, Department of Behavioral Sciences and Leadership, United States Military Academy, West Point; Dennis R. Kelly, Institutional Research and Analysis Branch, United States Military Academy, West Point, *Journal of Personality and Social Psychology*, 2007, Vol. 92, No. 6, 1087–1101. Copyright 2007 by the American Psychological Association.

[4] Mark Zuckerberg, https://www.facebook.com/zuck/posts/10101699265809491.

treating diseases through a program called Chan Zuckerberg Science. The money came from the $45 billion organization called the Chan Zuckerberg Initiative, which the couple started in 2015 to advance human potential and equality. This type of leadership inspires others to do good things as well.

Achieving valiant visionary status isn't reserved for those running billion-dollar companies. Imagine for a moment you've been hired to create your department. Ultimately, how would you like it to look? What would you like internal and external customers to say about their experience of working with you and your team? Remember, not all valiant visions have to be grand. Small—yet solid—steps that lead to results can be just as powerful as grand gestures.

# Five Things You *Must* Absolutely Do so You Can Move Ahead

You've picked up this book because you're interested in improving your leadership skills and moving your career forward. As you think about how to achieve continued success, think about the following.

## DEMONSTRATE COMPETENCE

The quickest way to advance your career is to demonstrate competence. You need to do this consistently. You may be a nice guy and you might know some well-connected people, but that won't mean a thing if you can't do your job well. When your boss makes a recommendation for a promotion, her reputation is on the line. She's not going to extend herself unless she is 100 percent sure you've got the right stuff to succeed.

## LET GO

This is the Monkey Bar Principle, which I learned from my mentor Alan Weiss. Some of you may recall playground stories from your parents about their adventures playing on the monkey bars, or perhaps you've had an opportunity to hang on these metal bars, swinging from one end of the play structure to the other. The key word here is *swinging*. You have to let go in order to move forward. I'll admit, I wasn't very good at this. I would hang in one place until I tired and found myself on the ground.

I learned some very valuable lessons on the playground, which can be applied to management. If you want to move ahead in the organization, you are going to have to let go of some of the things you are doing. Otherwise you'll tire out, and you will eventually fall down. This leads into the next point.

## DELEGATE

You won't be able to take on more interesting work if you don't learn how to delegate. I know what some of you micromanagers are thinking. "No one but me can do this task well." If that's the case, then move directly to my fourth tip, which is *hire right*, because obviously you don't have people on your team who are capable of handling day-to-day tasks. If that's not the case, then perhaps team members need additional training or you are in need of a coach to help you learn the art of delegation.

## HIRE RIGHT

The people who move up the quickest have demonstrated they are able to assemble and lead a great team of people. That's because management won't hesitate to promote you to a different position knowing you have a rock-solid team in place. Management knows your team will be able to continue their work successfully until a suitable replacement can be found to fill your position again. Keep this in mind as you look to hire your team. Before making an offer, ask yourself the following question: "Is this person good enough?" "Do they have the potential to be a strong team player?" If you hesitate, keep looking until such time as your response is, "Absolutely!"

## TRAIN YOUR REPLACEMENT

The most common reason I hear for holding back a promotion is that no one on the team can take this person's place. Is that fair? Maybe or maybe not. However, it's reality for many. If you want to move up in the organization, then make sure you train your replacement in advance. Some of you may be thinking this is a risky move. Won't they fire me and put this guy in my place for a lot less money? There's always a chance that could happen, but if it does then they've done you a favor, because this isn't the kind of company that puts people before profits. You now have the opportunity to take your talent to an organization that values people like you.

- Anyone can become a leader. The real differentiator is becoming the kind of leader others *want* to follow.
- Don't wait too long to ask for your next promotion. If you think you deserve it, ask for it!
- Signs you are ready for your next promotion include no longer feeling challenged, an opportunity falls into your lap, or you're having a hard time getting out of bed and coming to work.
- If the promotion doesn't go to you, don't despair. Ask your boss what you could have done differently to have earned the promotion. Make a decision as to whether you are going to stay and fully commit to your new boss or if you are going to leave. Or, seek another position in the organization.
- You can work toward securing the next promotion by practicing the things that make you most uncomfortable, following and learning from leaders you admire, becoming a thought leader yourself, connecting with other leaders, and adding value daily.
- There are a number of practices that distinguish great managers from the rest. Great leaders are lifetime learners. They are always looking to improve. They push the outer limits. They put people before personal gains and profits. They inspire others and bring out the best in people.
- To move ahead in your career, demonstrate competence, learn to let go, delegate, hire right, and train your replacement.

# References

Covey, Stephen M. R. 2009. "How the Best Leaders Build Trust." *Leadership Now*. www.leadershipnow.com/pvcovey.html (accessed on July 20, 2010).

de Gennaro, Renee, and John Kuchan. 2005. "The Power of Influence—Techniques for Leading When You're Not in Charge." http://pharmrep.findpharma.com/pharmrep/Sales+Training/The-power-of-influence/ArticleStandard/Article/detail/160220 (accessed on July 20, 2010).

Drucker, Peter. 1954. *The Practice of Management*. New York, NY: Harper and Row Publishers, Inc.

Klaus, Peggy. 2003. *Brag! The Art of Tooting Your Own Horn without Blowing It*. New York, NY: Warner Books, Inc.

Kotter, John P. 1985. *Power and Influence: Beyond Formal Authority*. New York, NY: The Free Press.

Lifland, Shari. 2006. "What, Me Brag?" American Management Association, August 10.

Mehrabian, Albert. Business model. http://www.businessballs.com/mehrabiancommunications.htm (accessed on July 20, 2010).

Pfeffer, Jeffrey. 1981. *Power in Organizations*. Cambridge, MA: Ballinger Publishing Co.

Schwartz, John, and Matthew L. Wald. 2003. "The Nation: NASA's Curse? 'Groupthink' Is 30 Years Old, and Still Going Strong." *New York Times*, March 9.

Tobak, Steve. 2010. "Undercover Boss: Escaping GM's Abusive Corporate Culture." BNET.com, March. http://blogs.bnet.com/ceo/?p=4254 (accessed on July 20, 2010).